Jury Thinking

JURY THINKING is the 2005 Companion Volume to
PRACTICAL JURY DYNAMICS © 2004 LexisNexis

new concepts, updates, practice tips,
& the 2005 *ABA Principles for Juries and Jury Trials*

by

Sunwolf, Ph.D., J.D.
Associate Professor
Santa Clara University

LexisNexis®

QUESTIONS ABOUT THIS PUBLICATION?

For CUSTOMER SERVICE ASSISTANCE concerning replacement pages, shipments, billing, reprint permission, or other matters,

please call Customer Service Department at 800-833-9844
email *customer.support@lexisnexis.com*
or visit our interactive customer service website at *www.lexisnexis.com/printcdsc*

For EDITORIAL **content questions** concerning this publication,

please call 800-446-3410 ext. 7447
or email: *LLP.CLP@lexisnexis.com*

For **information on other LEXISNEXIS MATTHEW BENDER publications**,

please call us at 800-223-1940
or visit our online bookstore at *www.lexisnexis.com/bookstore*

Cover illustration by W.B. Park. Contact Park-Art Studio, website: *www.wbpark.com*.

ISBN: 0-8205-8374-X

© 2005 Matthew Bender & Company, Inc., a member of the LexisNexis Group.

All rights reserved.

LexisNexis and the Knowledge Burst logo are registered trademarks, and Michie is a trademark of Reed Elsevier Properties Inc, used under license. Matthew Bender is a registered trademark of Matthew Bender Properties Inc.

LexisNexis®
Matthew Bender & Company, Inc.
Editorial Offices
P.O. Box 7587
Charlottesville, VA 22906-7587
800-446-3410
www.lexisnexis.com

Product Number 2460110

(Pub. 24600)

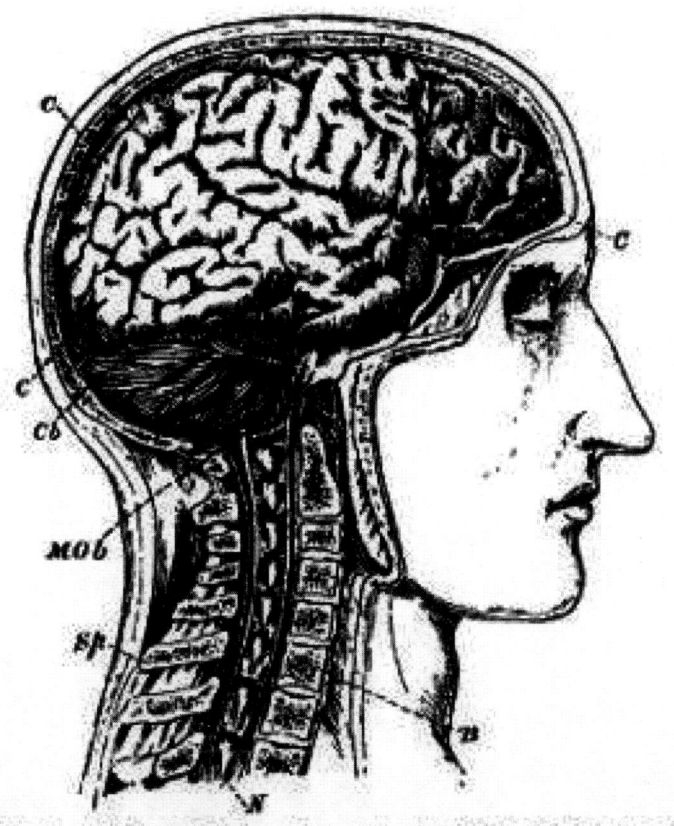

Side view of Human Brain and upper part of Spinal Cord, the skull and other coverings being removed.

C, C, C, cerebrum, or brain proper, showing the convoluted surface of the right cerebral hemisphere; *Cb*, cerebellum, or little brain — the striated surface of its right half; *MOb*, medulla oblongata; *N*, the spinal cord with beginnings of the spinal nerves; *B*, body of sixth cervical vertebra; *Sp*, its neural spine, or spinous process.

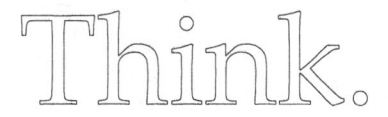

Think.

TABLE OF CONTENTS

Forethoughts ix

Chapter 1 BELIEFS AND THINKING 1
  § 1-1.   Biology of Beliefs 1
  § 1-2.   A Juror's TiVo® Mind 2
    § 1-2(a).   Automatic Search, Record, and Fast-forward Come Standard. . 3
    § 1-2(b).   Teaching Jurors How to Use their TiVo® Brains 4
  § 1-3.   Religious Beliefs 6
    § 1-3(a).   Differences that Make a Difference in Juror Thinking. 13
    § 1-3(b).   Juror Thinking about God and Science. 17

Chapter 2 THINKING UNAWARE 21
  § 2-1.   Blink 23
    § 2-1(a).   The Ick Factor 24
    § 2-1(b).   Juror Blink 26
    § 2-1(c).   Blink and Nonjurors 28
    § 2-1(d).   Issue-Specific Blink 30
    § 2-1(e).   Blink and Voir Dire 32
  § 2-2.   Mental Leaps 33
    § 2-2(a).   Expanding a Juror's Internal Thinking Criteria. 34
    § 2-2(b).   Creating Successful Mental Leaps. 35

Chapter 3 RE-THINKING 37
  § 3-1.   Juror Flipping 38
  § 3-2.   Ignoring Regret 42
  § 3-3.   If-Only Thinking 44
  § 3-4.   Binge-Think 46
    § 3-4(a).   Juror Thinking Binges 48
    § 3-4(b).   The Binge-Think Hangover 51
    § 3-4(c).   The Binge-Think Intervention 52

Chapter 4 SYMBOLIC THINKING 55
  § 4-1.   God Words and Devil Words 55
  § 4-2.   Metaphor and Thought 68
    § 4-2(a).   Metaphoric Thinking 69
    § 4-2(b).   Speaking in Metaphor 71
    § 4-2(c).   Types of Metaphoric Talk 72
    § 4-2(d).   Complex Metaphoric Phrases 76

Chapter 5	STRUCTURES THAT INFLUENCE THINKING	81
§ 5-1.	Jury Studies: Updates	81
§ 5-1(a).	Jury Instructions	82
§ 5-1(b).	Own Race Bias	82
§ 5-1(c).	Personal Injury Damage Awards	83
§ 5-1(d).	Expectation Effects	83
§ 5-1(e).	Lay Representations of Legal Concepts	83
§ 5-1(f).	Effect of Judicial Warnings During Trial	84
§ 5-1(g).	Reading Minds of Others (Mental States)	84
§ 5-1(h).	How Jurors Use/Misuse Character Evidence	84
§ 5-1(i).	Notetaking	84
§ 5-1(j).	Hearing and Believing Hearsay Evidence.	85
§ 5-1(k).	Juror Thinking About Witness Memory.	86
§ 5-1(l).	Effects of Defendant Conduct on Jury Thinking About Damage Awards.	88
§ 5-2.	Jury Reform	89
§ 5-2(a).	ABA 2005 Principles for Juries and Jury Trial	89
§ 5-2(b).	Reform Structures Missing from the ABA Principles	100
Chapter 6	IMPERFECT THINKING	105
§ 6-1.	Machine-Thinking	106
§ 6-2.	Wabi-Sabi Minds	107
§ 6-3.	Thinking in Paradox	109
§ 6-3(a). Unavoidable Paradox		109
§ 6-3(b). Paradox of Choice		110

2005 ABA Principles for Juries and Jury Trials	113
Browse the Stacks	137
Endnotes	139
Who Is the Author?	147
Index	149
Last Thought	163

Thoughts have power. Thoughts are energy.
You can make your world or break it, by your thinking.

—Susan L. Taylor, Editor-in-Chief, *Essence* Magazine

JURY THINKING

Forethoughts

> **NOT ALL BOOK SUPPLEMENTS SHOULD BE CUT FROM THE SAME TEMPLATE.** THIS MAY BE PARTICULARLY TRUE WHEN WE CHOOSE TO THINK ABOUT JURORS—SINCE EACH JUROR IS WONDERFULLY UNIQUE (AS IS EACH TRIAL). RATHER THAN OFFER SMALL INSERTS ACROSS A WIDE VARIETY OF SECTIONS IN THE ORIGINAL TEXT (NECESSITATING CONSTANT FLIPPING BACK AND FORTH), **JURY THINKING** IS FORMATTED AS A COMPANION, OFFERING NEW CONCEPTS, NEW PRACTICAL TIPS, UPDATES, AND, ESPECIALLY, NEW THINKING ABOUT JURORS.

JURY THINKING is the 2005 Companion Volume to PRACTICAL JURY DYNAMICS (LexisNexis 2004), a book that uniquely adopted both a "why-to" and a "how-to" approach to jury trial work. While many of the theories, concepts, and findings described *implicitly* suggested ways to more persuasively communicate with jurors, a variety of trial strategies were offered *explicitly*, to bring the concepts alive, in a practical way.

PRACTICAL JURY DYNAMICS also took an interdisciplinary perspective, drawing from communication, social psychology, behavioral neuroscience, linguistics, education, and the healing arts, to name a few.

JURY THINKING

> AMONG ECOLOGISTS, THERE IS A PRINCIPLE KNOWN AS **THE EDGE EFFECT**. THE EDGE EFFECT IS OBSERVABLE AT THE PLACE WHERE TWO DIFFERENT ECOLOGICAL COMMUNITIES (ECOSYSTEMS) SHARE A PHYSICAL BOUNDARY. THE RESULT IS AN AREA CREATED BETWEEN THE TWO, WHICH IS OF PARTICULAR RICHNESS AND DIVERSITY OF SPECIES.

New practical strategies offered here have been enriched by the intersecting edges of many disciplines and, consequently, they are the synergistic products of an Edge Effect.

THE CONCEPTS SHARED HERE ARE INTENDED TO GUIDE YOUR CHOICES AND TO BE ADAPTED BY YOU TO EACH UNIQUE CONTEXT, TRIAL, CLIENT, JUDGE, ISSUE, SITUATION, AND JUROR THAT YOU ENCOUNTER. THEY ARE NEVER TO BE FOLLOWED MINDLESSLY.

In JURY THINKING, a rich intersection is again explored that draws upon concepts and findings from law, jury research, group dynamics, social psychology, cognition, and neuroscience, so that these concepts are given an opportunity to talk to one another, in the context of *juries*.[1]

Trial advocacy, jury reform, and jury behavior texts, articles, and manuals generally give less attention to *three* critical areas that influence each Juror's Trial Task. The organization of PRACTICAL JURY DYNAMICS was designed to encourage more attention to a Juror's Trial World, in an original three-part sequence:

- **THE BIO-PHYSIOLOGY OF A JUROR'S BRAIN**

    (What are a juror's mental tools and limits?)

- **THE SOCIAL PSYCHOLOGY OF A JUROR'S PERCEPTIONS**

(How does a juror make sense of and evaluate the behaviors of other people?)

- **THE EFFECTS OF GROUP DYNAMICS ON A JUROR'S VOTE**

    (What happens when a juror becomes part of a group?)

---

[1]. A scholar of any particular discipline, as a result of their training, might find particular sections of this book either *naïve* or, on the other hand, *esoteric*. I acknowledge such criticism in advance—believing, nonetheless, that fresh interdisciplinary ideas can stimulate jury reform, trial practices, and jury research.

FORETHOUGHTS

Wherever you may currently be on your path as a trial practitioner, judicial administrator, consultant, or reformist, it is hoped that **JURY THINKING**, like PRACTICAL JURY DYNAMICS, will regularly invite your attention *differently*. This book invites ideas from domains that are not usually seatmates to the party.

> THE GOAL REMAINS THE SAME: TO HELP YOU SEE EACH JUROR IN MULTIPLE, DYNAMIC, FULL-COLOR DIMENSIONS—AS A COMPLETE HUMAN BEING.

Our courts at the highest levels have been, are, and ought to be, jury-oriented. This book offers *more* new knowledge for doing a better job.

Chapter 1

BELIEFS AND THINKING

Thinking about jury thinking is like wading through the complex maze of our own brain, in hopes of getting a clearer view of someone else's. The task is worthy, but challenging. Getting to the finish requires acknowledging and getting acquainted with a lot of dead-ends. A map would be useful—but mazes are mapless. There exist, however, useful patterns that are worth noticing.

§ 1-1. Biology of Beliefs

The brain's processes and tools are profoundly physical. While our beliefs may seem to flicker like candlelight and our opinions flash like drunken butterflies, our brain's *physical machinery* is producing each one. The human brain communicates with its partner, the body, in a stream of images and **back talk**. Back talking to ourselves, in fact, is the most frequent conversation any of us has with anyone. Studying the origin of consciousness, Julian Jaynes[1] suggested that originally when people received their brain's back talk, they

1

believed they were hearing voices inside their heads from otherworldly beings, telling them what to do.

Back talk both produces and reproduces beliefs. It is worth paying attention, then, to the *biology* of every juror's beliefs, because the brain's physical engine drives, *sub rosa*, a juror's judgments (see, The Bio-physiology of a Juror's Brain, Chapter 2 through Chapter 5, PRACTICAL JURY DYNAMICS). The human brain contains about 100 billion neurons, consumes a quarter of the body's oxygen, and spends most of the body's calories, while weighing only three pounds; in a single grain of brain sand, 100,000 neurons play at a billion synapses.[2] As a juror encounters new facts, new people, new situations, and new rules, that juror's neurons are firing more rapidly than when the juror experiences familiar places, performs familiar tasks, with familiar structures and known outcomes. The brain's neural reaction to novel situations is a circus of activity, since the neurons become excited. That neural "excitement" is, physically, what closes the synapses and sends information. Rapid back talk begins.

> Everyone is born a genius,
> but the process of living
> de-geniuses you.
> FOLKWISDOM

§ 1-2. A Juror's TiVo® Mind

A trial experience is like TiVo® for jurors.[3] While a juror's brain is more wonderful and impressive than the fanciest digital recording device ever devised, yet that brain is remarkably similar in function:

> Every juror's brain has been scanning, recording, replaying, and editing their experiences, since birth.

What a juror **believes** is a function of the settings of that juror's TiVo® brain. *Becoming aware of this built-in mechanism* is the first step to helping jurors manage their brains' TiVo® hardware, both during trial and during deliberations.

> GRAB THE REMOTE—IT TURNS OUT THERE ARE, INDEED,
> **TRIAL VIEWING OPTIONS** FOR A JUROR'S BRAIN.

BELIEFS AND THINKING

§ 1-2(a). Automatic Search, Record, and Fast-forward Come Standard

What is the *perceptual technology* of the brain that every juror has had since birth? Since the human brain attempts to organize the vast barrage of data that flings itself at us in every waking moment, "factory settings" are selected for numerous **mental filters** and **mental short cuts** (§ 7-1 and § 7-3, PRACTICAL JURY DYNAMICS). Our brains are doing their best to avoid the calamity of **message overload** (§ 2-3(b), PRACTICAL JURY DYNAMICS). Jurors, like all of us, are largely unaware of these settings or how they skew the data of life we store in our brains.

During trial, a juror's TiVo® brain (without being specifically asked) "knows" what that juror's preferences will likely be and scans the evidence and testimony to find "programs" that juror (based on past experiences) might like. *In other words, not everything during trial is getting recorded.*

The most likely events to be filtered out of our real world television TiVo® worlds are *advertisements*.

> **A JUROR'S TIVO® BRAIN WILL FILTER OUT ANYTHING PERCEIVED TO BE *SPONSORED ADS* DURING TRIAL—RECORDING ONLY EVENTS THAT SEEMS TO BE STRAIGHT INFORMATION OR ENTERTAINMENT.**

As a result, it is worth paying attention to the language we use, as lawyers, that signals to a juror, *"Now, a word from our sponsor."* Few jurors may be listening to that argument, witness, or demonstration. On the other hand, *"There's one thing you left out of your report, sir, isn't there?"* promises both information and drama. Listening happens—a juror's TiVo® brain doesn't register and scan out an "advertisement" that is interrupting the preferred program.

Early life experiences of abuse, abandonment, betrayal, exclusion, poverty, or struggle will set the brain's programming differently. Similarly, early life experiences of security, appreciation, accomplishments, loyalty, and inclusion set our brain's programming to recognize and expect that life has been that way for others. *Our perceptions are always only partly based on reality.* People emerge from childhoods that were blessed or cursed with caretakers; consequently the settings in our TiVo® brains vary considerably, yet, as adults, we remain unaware that we are actually *choosing* what to record and what our brains have edited out.

> **Practice Tip**: **Talk TiVo® to Jurors.**
>
> During jury selection, an attorney can raise awareness of the unconsciousness settings in our brains and still avoid glassy-eyed stares from a "brain cognition lecture" at the same time. Use TiVo® as the analogy:
>
> - How many of you have used TiVo®? [hands] How many are willing to admit, with me [your hand raised] they have TiVo® at home, but we leave it to someone else to do the settings? [hands, humor] What do you know about how it works? [call on someone] How does the Box seem to know what you want to watch? [Discussion]
>
> - Do you think that our brains might work a little bit like TiVo®? [call on a likely juror who could make that comparison] That's an interesting thought, isn't it?
>
> - If that's true, if our brains are scanning and editing, how could that be a little bit dangerous at trial, while jurors are listening to lots of evidence over many days? What could happen? [call on someone] What should we do about that? [collaborative discussion on how to listening differently, what to be aware of]
>
> - If that's true about our brains, do you think each juror might easily bring real different memories of the evidence into the jury room? It's only natural, right? [call on someone] What can we do about that? [collaborative suggestions]
>
> - Does it help, a little, to realize before deliberations that each of you is *scanning and recording the trial a little bit differently*? [call on several] How?

§ 1-2(b). Teaching Jurors How to Use their TiVo® Brains

When we are teaching jurors about how to consciously set their TiVo® Brains, keep in mind that we are also thinking about how to present evidence and argument in the courtroom that acknowledges that some settings for our jurors are stuck. **Voir dire**, in fact, can help us find out what the **mental pre-settings** are for these jurors and use our jury challenges more wisely.

TiVo® Thinking has a lot of explanatory power. Some of our cases need a lot of explaining. Here's a new way of thinking about the wonderful and frustrating TiVo® Brains of jurors, witnesses, judges, clients, advocates, and, yes, our relatives and, even, ourselves:

BELIEFS AND THINKING

> **TiVo® Brains in Court: A User's Guide[4]**
>
> 1. Notice existing settings.
> 2. Reset all preferences.
> 3. Learn the replay function.
> 4. Consciously push record!
> 5. Delete junk.
> 6. Fast-forward rarely.
> 7. Replay regularly (to see if it's actually working).
> 8. Recheck settings often.

There are myriad opportunities to help jurors understand and make better choices about their own TiVo® Brains. When deliberations become frustrating, some jurors may "get" why they all can't agree: they didn't record the same trial. This can lead to more compassionate listening to one another, as well as rethinking of positions.

> **Practice Tip: TiVo® Talk to Jurors about a Witness's TiVo® Brain.**
>
> Voir dire, opening statement, cross-examination, and closing argument are all excellent opportunities to point out the errors of someone's TiVo® Brain.
>
> - Prep jurors to look for (scan setting) the pre-settings that might explain why an eyewitness, doctor, company president, plaintiff have incompletely recorded an event in their memories. What got edited and why was that only natural?
> - Cross-examine witnesses using the TiVo® analogy, if you brought it up during jury selection. Jurors get it, it is accessible, and memorable.
> - Theme cases or issues around TiVo® analogies: No one noticed his TiVo® settings; the expert forgot to reset his preferences; she couldn't move off the replay function from long ago; he was always on fast-forward and, so, missed what really happened; too many people were messing with the settings.

The viewing options for jurors at trial can be both expanded and continually reset. In fact, they must be.

§ 1-3. Religious Beliefs

> The Brain—is wider than the Sky—
> For—put them side by side—
> The one the other will contain
> With ease—and you—beside
>
> The Brain is deeper than the sea—
> For—hold them—Blue to Blue—
> The one the other will absorb—
> As sponges—Buckets—do—
>
> The Brain is just the weight of God—
> For—Heft them—Pound for Pound—
> And they will differ—if they do—
> As Syllable from Sound—
>
> Emily Dickinson, 1862

Religious beliefs are never extraneous to a juror's thinking. The religious training and beliefs of every juror will unavoidably affect their thinking, especially in trials where a juror is invited to judge the behaviors of other people. Just as access to more than a single language helps us see the world in different ways, access to more than one understanding of spirituality and religion helps us imagine the thinking of each juror we may be trying to influence.

Even though it may seem that most Americans lead thoroughly secular lives, the United States claims to be deeply religious. According to a recent Gallup poll, 96% of Americans believe in "God, or a universal spirit," while 87% claim that religion is at least fairly important in their own lives.[5] *We may be a nation of believers, but most of us have no idea what our co-workers, neighbors, or friends believe in.*

In spite of the longstanding neglect jurors' religious beliefs have received from researchers and trial practice academies, new studies and thinking are pushing us in useful directions. In 2002 a powerful article, "Theology in the Jury Room: Religious Discussion as 'Extraneous Material' in the Course of Capital Punishment Deliberations"[6] appeared which invited us to expand our knowledge of the discussions behind the closed doors of many capital punishment jury rooms. Here, the impact of religious discussions during deliberations are acknowledged to be so strong that it is argued a court's jury instructions should address the inevitability of the topic. *What happens when secular jury thinking collides with religious jury thinking in the juryroom?*

The Bible may be the most imported book into jury deliberations of every type, civil or criminal. Bible-exposed jurors, when known, may result in an overturned verdict[7] or, on the other hand, labeled harmless error.[8] Clarence Darrow once argued in a confident generalization that Catholics made great jurors; now one legal scholar, Gerald F. Uelmen, takes a more recent view of the possible effects (for the juror as well as the case) of having a Catholic juror on a death penalty jury.[9] Several practical directions for more useful jury thinking emerge from Uelmen's article: (1) the argument that an attorney should be able to ask jurors about religion is grounded in the relevance of the question to discover bias or predisposition, (2) a juror's religious beliefs may lead to a challenge for cause or peremptory challenge, (3) the compartmentalization of religious beliefs from jury deliberations is impossible.

It is clear, as Uelmen asks us to notice, that the particular religious training of a Roman Catholic juror can impact the juror's decision-making thinking on a particular case and should be discussed during voir dire:

> Our Catholic juror could then be asked whether he or she agrees with the position espoused in the latest version of the Catholic Catechism, which says:
>
>> The traditional teaching of the Church does not exclude, presupposing full identity and responsibility of the offender, recourse to the death penalty, when this is the only practicable way to defend the lives of human beings effectively against the aggressor. If, instead, bloodless means are sufficient to defend against the aggressor and to protect the safety of persons, public authority should limit itself to such means, because they better correspond to the concrete conditions of the common good and are more in conformity to the dignity of the human person. Today, in fact, given the means at the State's disposal to effectively repress crime by rendering inoffensive the one who has committed it, without depriving him definitively of the possibility of

redeeming himself, cases of absolute necessity for suppression of the offender today are very rare, if practically non-existent.[10]

This excerpt from the Catholic Catechism, by itself, is enough to alert us to the fact that most of us are unfortunately ignorant of the doctrines of most religions in the world. A brief overview of some of the world religions with which we ought to become educated (whether we are attorneys, judges, or consultants) is offered here, in order to help organize our thinking about the constructs we need to know more about, should we find out the religion of any potential juror.

BELIEFS AND THINKING

Values and Beliefs of Eight Religious Orientations that May Influence Jurors[1]

	Buddhism	Chinese Religion	Christianity	Hinduism	Islam	Judaism	Scientology	New Age Spirituality
Law or Written Authority			Bible Gospel Scriptures	Dharma Four Vedas Bhagavad-Gita Mahabharata Law of Karma	Qur'an	Torah Talmud	Dianetics	
Historical Teachers	Buddha	Confucius	Jesus Christ Apostles	Shiva Vishnu Shakti Krishna Ram	Muhammad	Abraham Moses Solomon	L. Ron Hubbard	
Leader	Priest		Priest, Minister		Mullah	Rabbi, Rebbe		
Followers	Buddhist		Christian	Hindu	Muslim	Jew	Scientologist	
Values								
Precepts								
Virtues								
Sins								
Duties								
Death-Life Beliefs								
Violence Beliefs			You shall not kill. An eye for an eye.					
Derivative Sects	Theravada Mahayana	Taoism (Wisdom of Lao-tsu)	Roman Catholic, Orthodox, Episcopalian, Protestant, Anglican		Sufiism Sunni Shi'ites	Hasidic, Orthodox, Conservative, Reform, Liberal		Universalism Neo-paganism Wicca
Prevalence	300 million (Theravada: Sri Lanka, Burma, Thailand, Cambodia, Laos) (Mahayana: Vietnam, China, Korea, Japan, Tibet)	China	2 billion	800 million India	1.2 billion (South-East and Central Asia, India, Africa, Middle East, Turkey)	14 million		

---

1. *Religions are profound and complex spiritual belief systems that cannot be reduced to a table.* This chart is offered as a stimulus to your thinking about religious beliefs jurors may hold, offering categories and questions you should explore with religious leaders or practitioners to increase your understanding. **Blanks are created to emphasize that this is, at best, a worksheet in progress in your own thinking.** Fill in the blanks, but fill them in through thoughtful dialogue with other people. The information was used here was taken from a variety of Web sites.

JURY THINKING

Once we realize that the law says we are entitled to know the "scruples"[11] of any juror on any issue relevant to our trial, it is clear that unless we have a working knowledge of religious beliefs, the right to voir dire cannot be competently exercised. Uelmen reports that Minnesota upheld a prosecutor's peremptory challenge to a Jehovah's Witness,[12] Texas has affirmed a prosecutor's excusal of two Black jurors for being members of the Pentecostal church,[13] and a New Jersey court upheld the exclusion of a Black Muslim from a jury.[14]

> **Practice Tip: Gather the case law on jurors and religion.**
>
> Uelmen's article and its citations are an excellent start. The right to voir dire or have a questionnaire that addresses a juror's religious training, strength of belief, and religious practices can arise at any time in trial. The cases that have addressed jurors and religion (including religious icons, books, and teachings in the jury room) are needed in the trial resources tool box.

How seriously a juror takes their own religious dogma is more important than the religion they claim. Some people are actually ignorant of the dogma of the religion they claim; others are not. An effective trial advocate must be able to intelligently distinguish between fundamentalists, reformists, and occasional believers. Current or regional issues are effective tools for unearthing these qualities:

> **Practice Tip: What do you think about that?**
> - What are your thoughts about private religious schools for children?
> - What are your thoughts about requiring employers to honor all religious holidays of employees?
> - What are your thoughts about whether the Ten Commandments should be displayed in courthouses?
> - What are your thoughts about religious displays of the manger and baby Jesus in front of courthouses at Christmas?
> - Would you want to know a person's religion before you accepted them as a juror in a case that was important to you?

BELIEFS AND THINKING

> - Whatever the answer of a juror, the follow up question to all of the above must be, "Why?" and the follow up question to the reason must be, "Can you give us an example?"
> - It was recently reported that one of the jurors on a death penalty murder trial wanted to consult with his priest before indicating whether he could be fair. What are your thoughts about that juror's request? Should *devout* jurors consult with their religious leaders, before they can truly say whether they can serve on a jury? [Why or why not?]

Some jurors are biased against religions outside their own, and other jurors hold strong ideas about what members of another religion believe or how they behave (even if they are wrong). Your client's religion, your religion, a witness's perceived religion may influence that juror.

The most useful Practice Tip that can be offered, as a result, is to research the religious groups in the community where your trial is taking place. Here's a practical glimpse of religious groups in the United States from adherents.com:

- In 2002, the top twenty religions in the United States were:[15]

Christianity	76.5%
Nonreligious	13.2%
Judaism	1.3%
Buddhism	0.5%
Agnostic	0.5%
Atheist	0.4%
Hinduism	0.4%
Unitarian/Universalist	0.3%
Wiccan/Pagan/Druid	0.1%
Spiritualist	0.05%
Native American	0.05%
Baha'i	0.04%
New Age	0.03%
Sikhism	0.03%
Scientology	0.02%
Humanist	0.02%
Deity/Deist	0.02%
Taoist	0.02%
Eckankar	0.01%

In fact, a working knowledge of the various religious groups within Christianity eludes most of us. Consider that Christianity includes some divergent seatmates:

> Catholic, Baptist, Protestant, Methodist, Wesleyan, Lutheran, Presbyterian, Pentecostal/Charismatic, Episcopalian, Anglican, Mormon/Latter-day Saints, Church of Christ, Jehovah's Witness, Seventh-Day Adventist, Assemblies of God, Holiness, congregational/United Church of Christ, Church of the Nazarine, Church of God, Eastern Orthodox, Evangelical, Mennonite, Christian Science, Church of the Brethren, Born Again, Non-denominational Christians, Disciples of Christ, Reformed, Dutch Reformed, Apostolic, New Apostolic, Quaker, Full Gospel, Christian Reform, Foursquare Gospel, Fundamentalist, Salvation Army, Independent Christian Church, Covenant Church, Jewish Christians, *to name a few*.

Practice Tip: Map the religious groups in your jurisdiction.

- Where are the places of worship (neighborhoods)?
- What is the membership?
- Who are the religious leaders?
- What are the recent homilies, sermons offered (frequently publicly posted)?
- What are the days of worship?
- What ethnicities are included?
- What community projects does the group devote itself to? [Extends the map to the other groups that connect or are benefited by this religious group.]
- Does it have any private schools?

As previously suggested, more investigation is useful concerning the doctrine of the religious group, however, a neighborhood map that reflects socio-economic, ethnic, geographic, topical issues is valuable to develop a richer understanding of the role of that group in the community of the trial.

BELIEFS AND THINKING

§ 1-3(a). Differences that Make a Difference in Juror Thinking

The religious thinking of potential jurors and sworn-in jurors challenges the thinking of attorneys and judges and, to date, has dwelled in the shadows of trial advocacy. Religious jurors, however, offer an important *dialectic*—that is, something that forces us to grapple with two seemingly contradictory possibilities.

> A JUROR'S RELIGIOUS THINKING BOTH CONSTRAINS AND EXPANDS THE POSSIBILITIES OF COURTROOM PERSUASION.

How does this happen? Previously, practical thinking about the effects of a juror's **value system** has been discussed (§ 8-9, Cracked Perceptual Lenses, PRACTICAL JURY DYNAMICS). Values are those **mental-rulers** people hold about what behaviors should be applauded or punished. The religious beliefs of a juror will always be the unconscious or conscious "default" mode a juror returns to when thinking about the evidence, when a more appropriate "ruler" is not offered (or accepted).

- A juror's religious thinking **constrains** the possibilities of courtroom persuasion because it is difficult, if not impossible, to override a personal religious belief. As a result, it is wise to assume that a juror's religious training creates structured *walls* within which a juror will be thinking about every aspect of the trial.

- A juror's religious thinking simultaneously **expands** the possibilities of courtroom persuasion because pre-existing beliefs offer valuable *markers* for framing issues within a trial that will be more readily accepted and "make sense" for a juror. Further, a juror can more readily argue a case to other jurors (deliberation) if that juror is given a bridge to personal pre-existing religious thinking.

Below is offered some of the fundamental differences in religious thinking that will not be immediately apparent to a lawyer or judge on the outside of the vernacular.[16]

> ### A GUIDE TO RELIGIOUS THINKING ABOUT JURORS[2]
> ### (MAKING SENSE OF DIFFERENCES THAT MIGHT MATTER)
>
> - **Charismatics**: Appearing initially in California in the 1960s, derived from the Pentecostals, but differed by placing less emphasis on "speaking in tongues" (glossolalia). Cherish "gifts of the Spirit" in a variety of forms. Emphasizes a personal relationship with Jesus Christ, shaped by Bible study, prayer, and evangelistic fervor, spreading throughout Christian sects including the Catholic Church.
>
> - **Cursillo®**: Appeared in the 1950s, now used to help Roman Catholics grow closer to God through a three-day event emphasizing conversation and prayer. Alumni meet to pray and evangelize. The National Cursillo Center has a major web site explaining the movement at www.natl-cursillo.org. Strong belief that the mystery of God cannot be explained, but there is an attempt to use evangelization as a natural act of being Christlike during everyday activities.
>
> - **Evangelicalism**: [Term originates in the Greek word "evangelion" or "the good news" or gospel.] The Protestant movement in which members are *born again* or "saved." Followers witness their faith to others, convert nonbelievers, stress the importance of Scripture, and seek to develop a closer relationship with God. Four hallmarks of evangelical religion are *conversionism* (belief that lives need to be changed), *activism* (expressing the gospel in acts), *Biblicism* (regard for the teachings of the Bible), and *crucicentrism* (a stress on the sacrifice of Christ on the cross).
>
> - **Fundamentalism**: Known as a more conservative form of evangelicalism whose followers believe in the Bible as the literal sacred word of God. Fundamentalists see themselves as the guardians of the truth, to the exclusion of others' interpretation of the Bible. Most members are socially and politically conservative and adopt strict personal moral codes.

---

2. Necessarily truncated, this Guide does not intend to short-change or properly represent any of the followers described. Rather, it is intended as a guide to prod more in-depth research and thinking about the diversity of religious vernacular aspects of believers in our jury pools. It suggests that there are differences among followers of these groups that *will significantly matter to how a juror thinks about* adversaries, witnesses, issues, blame, events, behaviors, injuries, remedies, causation, and legal principles.

- **Hasidism**: ["Hasid" means "pious" used to designate one whose devotion extends beyond the technical requirements of Jewish religious law.] A branch of the Orthodox Jewish movement, emphasizing devotion and direct, emotional worship of God. Hasidim pray ecstatically, dance with Torah, and fast to achieve a higher spiritual state. Members conform to various customs of dress modeled on 18th-century Russian village life. Principal teachings include: priority of emotion over intellect, overwhelming consciousness of God's presence in all things, a consciousness of profound joy, evil differs from good only by degree (sinner always has the potential for self-improvement and is never rejected by a compassionate God), prayer, and love of Israel as an ideal solidarity with fellow Jews.

- **Kabbalah**: ["Kabbalah" is derived from the root "to receive, to accept."] A mystical segment of Judaism that studies esoteric writings in early Jewish texts (Zohar, a 13th century Aramaic text) in order to determine hidden meanings in Torah, historically emerging from 12th century France. Active speculation on the nature of divinity, creation, the origin and fate of the soul, and the role of humans. Devotional and magical practices taught only to a select few are preserved. Hollywood-inspired groups (Madonna) may be more pop-oriented, wearing red string bracelets, viewed as protection against spiritual and social negative forces in the world around us (ill will) that block us from realizing our full potential.

- **Paganism**: Originating in pre-Christian parts of Europe and Great Britain, today's followers incorporate early practices into modern-day rituals, such as festivals (Solstice, Equinox, All Hallo's Eve, all centered on *nature* as inspiration for and embodiment of spirituality. Belief that everything has a spirit, and many believe in reincarnation of the spirit after death, rather than heaven or hell.

- **Pentecostalism**: A form of Christianity originating in Kansas around 1900, which emphasizes baptism in the Holy Spirit, a direct experience of God, speaking in tongues, and prohibitions on such modern activities as dancing. Focus on empowerment, with subgroups (Church of God, International Church of the Four-square Gospel, International Pentecostal Holiness Church, Assemblies of God). Experience, rather than doctrine, is the principal determinant of Pentecostalism. Speaking in tongues is viewed as a miraculous act in which a believer possessed of the Holy Spirit speaks in a language without having knowledge of it.

> Also believe in the "casting out of devils" (exorcism), shouting, and being "slain in the Spirit" which are observed with great zeal.
>
> - **Sufism**: [*tasawwuf*, as it is called in Arabic] Generally understood to be the inner, mystical, psycho-spiritual dimension of Islam, though today many Muslims believe that Sufism is outside the sphere of Islam. Emerging from Islam in the Middle East in the 7th century, a tradition that seeks intimacy with the divine through contemplation, story-teaching, and everyday wisdom. Essential teaching that the Sufi surrenders to God, in love, over and over, which involves embracing with love at each moment the content of one's consciousness (perceptions, thoughts, feelings, sense of self) as manifestations of God.
>
> - **Wicca**: A neopagan, earth-centered religion. Known as the largest branch of Paganism in the United States, members have been referred to by outsiders as witches (to insiders as a Wiccan, or Neopagans) and follow a code of personal freedom, responsibility, and respect for nature. Some of the growth of the movement today is seen among teenagers rejecting the autocracy and insensitivity to the environment that they believe is part of traditional religions.
>
> - **Zen**: Dating to the 520s in China, a derivative philosophical root of Buddhism that focuses on meditation in search of personal enlightenment. Life is seen as a tough but not scientific adventure or a product of rational mind. The Zen belief is that any person is able with training to reach total absorption or personal enlightenment. Zen cannot be learned by traditional study, but everyday practice; it is not a system of articulated beliefs or scriptures, but a structured system of behaviors or practices. Three components of Zen practice are *zazen* (sitting meditation), *koan* (unsolvable riddle), and *sanzen* (dialogue with the Zen master).

Even a cursory reading of the above "guide" showcases a vast treasure of **differences that will make a difference in a juror's thinking in the courtroom**. Some belief systems have clear implications for how a juror would think in cases that have issues involving the environment, resources, property, or animals. Others have clear implications for how a juror might think in cases that will rely upon science, testing, laboratory work, and experts. Add to this that some of these groups have strong feelings about the role of women, the rules of marriage, and the possibility of forgiveness. *Imagine, further, how jurors from different belief systems might receive one another's reasoning during deliberations!*

BELIEFS AND THINKING

§ 1-3(b). Juror Thinking about God and Science

Recently, *a collision between science and religion* has inundated the news, as well as courtrooms across the country:

Should a courthouse display the Ten Commandments?

May a judge display and speak his or her own religious views in court?

Must a witness take an oath on the Bible?

Is stem cell research a violation of God's commandment, "Thou shalt not kill?"

Must "intelligent design" be taught in schools along with evolution?

Should private religious schools receive government funding?

As a result, both ordinary and prominent people are beginning to speak out about their faith in a variety of venues. At a recent scientific conference at City College in New York, a member of the audience asked the esteemed scientists, who were all *Nobel laureates*, "Can you be a good scientist and believe in God?" Herbert Hauptman (chemistry prize, 1985) replied that belief in God is like belief in the supernatural and was incompatible with good science, declaring, "This kind of belief is damaging to the well-being of the human race."

> CLEARLY, WE ARE NOT ALL ON THE SAME PAGE WHEN IT COMES TO THE COMPATIBILITY OF RELIGION AND SCIENCE. JURORS MAY NOT EVEN BE READING FROM THE SAME BOOK.

Many religious people believe that science is a godless endeavor and that scientists are themselves contemptuous of God-fearing people. Some jurors would believe that a scientist's moral values would affect their work.

Practice Tip: Current Issues as a Barometer of Juror Thinking

- Use the six questions above to stimulate jurors to reveal their own thinking and level of tolerance. Either questionnaires or oral voir dire are appropriate.

- Any case in which science will be offered as evidence or contested is sufficient justification for exploring, in depth, a juror's religious beliefs.

> - Develop a file on the religious groups in your judicial district. Research on the Internet the Web sites for each and develop supporting documents you can offer the court to show why a juror who is a member of that group would be the basis for a potential challenge for cause (beliefs contrary to the law in this case) or would be the basis for you to exercise a peremptory challenge based upon the centrality of certain issues to your client's case.

We need to have better tools for unearthing a juror's religious thinking.

> **Practice Tip: New Questions on a Juror's Religious Practices**
>
> Here are some possibilities to stimulate your thinking. These are appropriate for jury questionnaires.
>
> - Have you or your children ever attended a religious school or college?
> - Do you practice any religion?
> - In what religion were you raised?
> - Have you converted from one religion to another?
> - Have you left any religion that you once belonged to?
> - Do you consider yourself to be religious?
> - Do you belong to a church, synagogue, mosque, or house of worship?
> - Do you have any relatives or friends that hold a position of leadership in any religion?
> - Have you ever experienced a personal relationship with God?
> - Do you believe in heaven or hell?
> - What are your thoughts about reincarnation?
> - Do you have any daily practices that are important to your own religious beliefs?
> - Which two religious leaders in the world do you most admire?
> - In what religion have you raised your children?
> - Did you marry outside your religion?
> - Are there any religious groups with which you strongly disagree?
> - What are your beliefs about people who do not belong to your religion?

> - What limitations or restrictions does your religion have for women?
> - Would prayer be a part of your role as a juror? Give an example.
> - Have you attended services in other religions? Which ones?
> - What is the biggest religious issue in our country today, in your mind, that involves the role of religion?

Rich metaphors, parables, and analogies between the people in your case and the historical people in a juror's religion can be made. Suzannah and the Elders, from the Christian Bible, offers a story about the first motion to sequester witnesses and the difficulty of determining who is telling the truth; see also King Solomon and the two women claiming the same baby. The struggles of Israel's King David have been compared to the trials of today's young people who are besieged by violence, drugs, and sexual temptations. Jurors may see a trial as one of spiritual warfare, evil versus good, or the prodigal son returning. When we allow ourselves to explore someone else's religious beliefs *before we enter the courtroom*, we have the opportunity to learn the language that can best influence that juror's thinking about our case. Go to someone else's place of worship. More than once. There are wonders to be seen.

As pointed out, many trials you are involved in may involve issues that will be impacted by a juror's religious beliefs. At a practical level, there is a need to get a broad spectrum of information about a juror's religious beliefs, without using a lot of questionnaire space.[3] Here is one example of how that could be accomplished (allowing oral voir dire for follow up questioning). These are questions that could be offered by the court, *sua sponte*, or attorneys. The **column format**, on a written questionnaire, is visually appealing to jurors (allowing them to quickly see the distinctions you are asking them to make). The compact nature of the format is visually easier to *assess* for lawyers reviewing the jurors' answers:

---

3. Legal basis for questions: These questions are essential for the attorney to intelligently exercise peremptory challenges, to effectively develop legal challenges for cause, and to provide effective assistance of counsel under both the state and federal constitutions. A denial of the right to receive answers to any of these questions would substantially impair the party's right to due process of law and a fair trial, under both the state and federal constitutions. These questions are further essential to obtaining and preserving a record on appeal on the issues presented during jury selection concerning requests for in-chambers questioning of certain jurors, the exercise of challenges, requests for additional challenges, and/or the request for additional time to talk to specific jurors.

JURY THINKING

Sample Questionnaire on Religion

Your answers to the questions below are important and will help the attorneys decide who should serve as jurors on this particular trial. The court will protect your questionnaires and preserve the confidentiality of your answers.

- *[This case involves key issues, roles, and practices in the Catholic church.]*
- *[This case involves deeply held moral values and beliefs.]*
- *[This case involves the choices and behaviors of people who may hold a different religion than you or your family.]*
- *[This case involves issues about science and scientists that may be impacted by a juror's religious beliefs.]*
- As a result, it is important that the attorneys have information about the religious background, training, and affiliations of potential jurors. Please tell us:

The religion of each of your **parents**:	The religion you *currently* **most closely identify yourself with**:	**Past religions** you have identified with—that are **no longer your religion**:	The religion of your **husband or wife**, if you are married (or engaged to be married):	Religion you are raising (or raised) your **children** in:

A juror's religion should not be a taboo subject in the courtroom, but it has been.

"Where is God?"
[Call of Teller to Audience]
"We don't know—but the Stories do!"
[Response of Audience to Teller]

—Traditional call and response in continental Africa, seeking of and granting of permission to begin the storytelling.

Chapter 2

THINKING UNAWARE

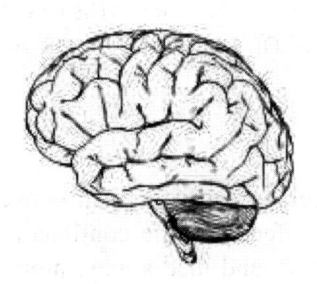

> The more you learn about the brain's architecture, the more you recognize that what happens in your head is more like an orchestra than a soloist, with dozens of players contributing to the overall mix.
>
> —Steven Johnson, *Mind Wide Open*[17]

> Imagine the brain, that shiny mound of being, that mouse-gray parliament of cells, that dream factory, that petit tyrant inside a ball of bone, that huddle of neurons calling all the plays, that little everywhere, that fickle pleasuredrome, that wrinkled wardrobe of selves stuffed into the skull like too many clothes into a gym bag.
>
> —Diane Ackerman, *An Alchemy of Mind*[18]

People do not always *speak their minds*, even when it might benefit them to do so. It is suspected in addition, however, that people do not usually *know their minds*. **What happens when deliberations consists of some jurors who will not speak their minds, together with a lot of jurors who do not know their minds?**

The mental processes of learning and deciding are largely invisible to us. Our brain's cognitive-thinking activities take place at high speed, on multiple simultaneous levels, and are continual. This **thinking unaware**, or mindspinning, is difficult, if not impossible, to turn off (§ 2-2, PRACTICAL JURY

DYNAMICS). Further, each juror has a tolerance for receiving new information that differs, in important ways, from that of other jurors.

> THE SPEED AND FORMAT OF THE NEW INFORMATION WE SEND TO JURORS WILL DETERMINE, IN PART, THE DEGREE TO WHICH THEY ARE ABLE TO MAKE SENSE OF IT, STORE IT, OR ACCURATELY RETRIEVE IT LATER.

Jury studies are now seeking to distinguish between individual jurors based upon **media socialization** effects. Media continually socialize people to *prefer how they receive information*, and media may, more alarmingly, disable people from receiving information in other formats.

It has been suggested that **Generation X jurors** (those born between 1966 and 1981) and **Generation Y jurors** (those born in 1982 or later) have been immersed in and exposed to receiving new facts in ways that significantly challenge trial advocates (and judges). Generation X and Y jurors were raised on computers, video games, the Internet, and an infinite variety of programming available on cable television. As a result, the traditional lecture-format opening or closing statement may cause them to zone out, notwithstanding linguistic eloquence.

More senior jurors, on the other hand, were raised on newspapers and magazines; some still subscribe to and read them everyday. In short, a **book-reading juror** will process and receive literary-style information (lectures, tables, documents) with more ease and familiarity than an **Internet-video juror**. Generation X and Y jurors, however, who are socialized by truncated media bites, google searches, and web popovers/popunders, value their own snap judgments. They are often willing to let a little bit of knowledge go a long way:

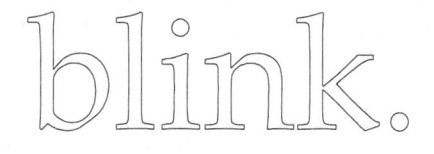

blink.

THINKING UNAWARE

§ 2-1. Blink

"I'm going to ask the jury to hold its applause until all the evidence has been introduced."

© The New Yorker Collection 1995 Michael Maslin from cartoonbank.com. All Rights Reserved.

A juror's mind is both fast and frugal, not only **mind-spinning**, but also seeking **short-cuts** (§ 7-3, PRACTICAL JURY DYNAMICS). The human mind loves hunches, the law does not.

A **juror hunch** occurs regularly during the juror's trial task because the brain loves to leap to conclusions, rather than wade through unfamiliar murky places. In short, a juror hunch is the modern manifestation of the evolutionary adaptive unconscious, acting like a giant computer that quickly and quietly processes a lot of novel data.[19] The brain's decision-making parts are capable of making quick judgments based on little information when sizing up the world, in order to warn us of danger: this is a good thing. However, making quick judgments when listening to complex trial evidence in bits and pieces, frequently out of order: not so much.

Malcolm Gladwell's **blink**[20] is an extraordinarily useful concept for understanding and strategizing about the **snap judgment** functioning of a juror's thinking brain. In the everyday world, "snap judgment" carries a negative connotation (as in, *"Hold on, don't make any snap judgments, here."*). We assume that the quality of a decision is directly related to the time and effort that went into making it. *Haste makes waste. Don't judge a book by its cover.* What if, instead, some of a juror's most profound judgments during trial are the products of rapid cognition (snap judgments)? What if, further, a juror's spontaneous impressions and conclusions about a new person or complex situation happen in *two seconds*?

The **Theory of Thin Slices** explains how our frugal brains are willing to let a little bit of knowledge go a long way. One critical aspect of rapid thinking is known as thin-slicing.

> THIN-SLICING DESCRIBES THE ABILITY OF OUR BRAINS TO FIND PATTERNS IN SITUATIONS AND BEHAVIORS, BASED ON NARROW SLICES OF EXPERIENCE OR INFORMATION.

The BLINK! factor and thin-slicing offer two provocative counter-intuitive thoughts for trial lawyers:

- Decisions a juror makes in two-seconds can be every bit as good as decisions made cautiously, after thoughtful deliberation.
- A juror's snap judgments and first impressions can be educated and controlled.

BLINK! and **thin-slicing** are, in other words, practical cognitive tools.

§ 2-1(a). The Ick Factor

The BLINK! judgment that may be most familiar to trial attorneys comes from certain facts in a case: the disgusting ones. Some trial facts are *repulsive*, either physically or morally. Think of this as the *Ick Factor*. "Ick" appropriately captures the mental judgment a person makes, in two seconds, about that fact.

The Ick Factor kicks in when the fast and frugal thinking of *most people* to that fact produces the reaction: "ick." When people have uneven or broad spectrum reactions to this fact, there is no Ick Factor (only, perhaps an individualized yuck). The Ick Factor kicks in for a lawyer, a judge, an expert, a witness *immediately*. Two seconds. Thoughtful cognitive reflection bypassed. Hence, the Ick Factor (a profound thinking judgment of a juror) will occur when repulsive trial facts come into evidence.

> IT IS THE JOB OF THE TRIAL LAWYER TO NEUTRALIZE THE ICK FACTOR WHEN IT HURTS A CLIENT AND TO SHOWCASE THE ICK FACTOR WHEN IT HELPS A CLIENT.

When we read about someone else's case in the news, our own two-second blink thinking kicks in and we are immediately aware of the Ick Factor: flesh-eating virus, a dead kitten, a dog mauling, incest, sex in a church, baby dangling from window, slimy things, filthy things, cruel things.

> **Practice Tip**: Train yourself to **scan for the Ick Factor** the *first time* you meet a client or receive a case. Your brain's two-second reactions are initial data.
>
> Consider, then, my four tactics for dealing with bad facts:
>
> 1. Attempt to suppress it. [What motions can I file?]
> 2. Neutralize it to the jury. [Who cares?]
> 3. Use it in your favor. [But that also means ...]
> 4. Deny it. [Who says?]
>
> - First, look for legal reasons an Ick Fact should not be admitted at all (procedural violations, tainting, chain-of-custody, constitutional violations, balancing test for prejudicial effect or probative value).
>
> - That failing, fold the Ick Fact into your case theme, by neutralizing it for the jury—so they realize that it won't help them analyze *the issue in dispute* ("Yes, he signed the contract, but that doesn't tell you what he understood or what he had been told that meant.").
>
> - Third, consider using an Ick Fact in your favor ("Yes, she shot him six times, which demonstrates how emotional/psychotic she was, because the first shot did the trick.")
>
> - Finally, all else failing, consider the efficacy of denying an Ick Fact by attacking its source (who heard it, saw it, claims to know) and the reliability of the testimony (Was it recorded at a later time, could it have been audio-taped or video-taped but wasn't, was it seen by more than one person, were notes destroyed, was it mentioned originally?). This is the familiar childhood, "Did too, did not," strategy—*just because a witness says it happens, doesn't mean a juror must believe it.*

JURY THINKING

§ 2-1(b).   Juror Blink

"I still say you never can tell which way a jury will go."

© The New Yorker Collection 1989 Frank Modell from cartoonbank.com. All Rights Reserved.

Jurors thin slice **witnesses** as they take the stand, gain powerful blink impressions of **attorneys** before they are introduced, and draw conclusions about **other jurors** in seconds. These impressions can be problematic in a trial, where the judicial system wants the jurors to consider all of the evidence, together with all of the law—not thin slice it. BLINK! factors must, as a result, be anticipated and accounted for by lawyers.

Practice Tip: Jury priming.

Once we acknowledge that juror Blink! will happen in the courtroom, it is clear that the power of first impressions privileges direct examination. Contaminating a witness's credibility, attitude, motive on cross-examination may be too late. If a witness is likely to create a great impression (such as a young child or well-published expert) on direct examination, opening statement should be used to re-frame the witness's attitude, motive, weaknesses, character, bias—before direct examination. Cross-examination is evidence, so present your questions and anticipated answers, along with the anticipated attitude of the witness, during your

> opening. Some jurors will develop an impeaching Blink! about that witness before direct examination. Cross-examine critical witnesses before cross-examination, during opening.

During deliberations, it may be that a juror has difficulty explaining how she *knows* to other jurors. The BLINK! factor offers a powerful explanation for this aspect of juror thinking. Knowing is one thing, explaining it to others is another; this is particularly frustrating when a juror is not in the majority. The *erroneous presupposition* is that any juror owes it to the other jurors to clearly explain how they *know*, offering specifics in support. [Jump here, for a moment, to the description below about Bird Watcher Blink, § 2-1(c).] Blink theory says this kind of explaining cannot really be done when the process of knowing was not slow rationality, and, further, that sometimes a juror cannot figure out *how* he knows, let alone explain it to others.[21]

Surprisingly, in fact, two professors from Columbia University discovered that if you make people explain themselves about blink judgments, something strange happens. What once seemed clear becomes suddenly confusing.[22]

> **Practice Tip: Arm jurors to honor their personal blinks during deliberations.**
>
> By closing argument you may have a clearer idea whether a blink impression may have helped or hurt you during a particular trial. It would be hard to predict in advance. Alert jurors to it and, if it may have helped because what you are hoping for would be difficult to put into words, remind jurors that they can say to one another, *"I feel strongly about that, but cannot explain it further."*

Sometimes it is clear that a lot of blinking may happen in your trial, so talking to jurors about it during voir dire and exercising your peremptory challenges as a result of those conversations (attorneys blink jurors on too little information all the time, which does not make the judgment erroneous), is appropriate:

> **Practice Tip: Disable Juror Blink.**
>
> Two-second impressions don't ALWAYS yield accurate judgments. Our brain's computer is fallible at times, when it attempts to rapidly decode a novel situation. When a juror is *distracted*, blink is most likely to be thrown off (see the Bio-physiology of Divided Attention, § 2-3(c), PRACTICAL JURY DYNAMICS).
>
> - Add to your challenge for cause arguments to the court the information about juror blink for a juror who has many distracting events happening in their life that need their attention.
>
> - Talk to the jurors, as a whole, during voir dire, about **jury blink** and ask them how they might go about disabling it for themselves. This should be a **collaborative discussion** (*How can we solve this interesting natural thing our brains do?*), rather than an admonition, warning, or lecture. Giving jurors a glimpse of **blink** (with any luck, some juror has read the best-selling book) is interesting for them. It's about their own wonderful brains:
>
>   - "There's something that might influence your verdict, other than the law or the evidence, and I want to ask you about that. Scientists who study the human brain say there is a Blink Factor, where we make judgments about someone new in two-seconds. Do you have an example of that? Is that something you've noticed?"
>
>   - "We all do it, but it's dangerous at trial. Why might it be dangerous, in your opinion?"
>
>   - "When one side has to wait to cross-examine, or wait to call a witness, the Blink Factor may mean jurors have already made a judgment they are not even aware of."
>
>   - "How would you suggest we disable the blink factor in this trial?"

§ 2-1(c).   Blink and Nonjurors

Blink is not just for jurors. Blink, in fact, has a lot of **explanatory power** when our task is to explain human behavior to others. In a single trial, the blink factor may be able to do a lot of explaining for trial lawyers. In both civil and criminal cases, there may be: ATTORNEY BLINK, DOCTOR BLINK, EXPERT BLINK, COP BLINK, BLINK DIAGNOSES, WITNESS BLINK, OR CORPORATE BLINK. It is worth applying the blink factor to events in the trial to see whether richer explanations can be offered to jurors about behaviors, decisions, and impressions that are the focus of the controversy:

- Consider **the blink factor and physicians**, as one robust example. Attorneys defending physician choices and behaviors can use the studies about accurate blink and physician training to help jurors judge a physician's rapid fire diagnosis as reliable. Attorneys attacking physician choices or behaviors will want to expose the fallibility of blink.

- Intriguing, for medical malpractice lawyers of either side, is **patient blink**. The risk of being sued for malpractice has little to do with how many mistakes a doctor makes, since the overwhelming number of people who suffer an injury due to physician negligence never file a malpractice suit at all. Some patients file lawsuits because of the blink factor that occurs in their relationship with the doctor. Shoddy medical care + patient blink about how they were treated personally. Plaintiffs say they were ignored, rushed, talked to rudely or condescendingly, or treated poorly. Patients sue doctors they don't like and liking a doctor happens during the unconscious blink factor moments.[23] When a physician does not explain or listen, **blink happens** as the patient is escorted out of the office. (Rarely does a plaintiff come to a lawyer to say, "I feel terrible about this because I really like this doctor, but I want to sue her.") In fact, trial bar members can regale you with frustrating tales of plaintiffs who refused to add doctors or nurses to the lawsuit even when discovery disclosed negligent acts: "I don't care, I love her and I'm not going to sue her.")[24] Jurors may thin-slice a doctor on the witness stand and find her wanting before the key questions are asked or answered.

- Blink skill is essential for professional **athletes**, explaining the ability of players who can take in and comprehend all that is happening around them in two seconds and choose accordingly, without conscious reflection.

- In the **military**, the brilliance of military leaders has been attributed to an ability to know at a glance the sense of the battlefield.

- **Bird watchers** rely on blink in making identifications. The moment for spotting a bird in flight may be fleeting, not long enough for careful identification; however, the experienced birder gets the "gist" or essence of the bird and "knows." Ornithologist David Sibley explains that a sense of how a bird moves from quick flashing sequences, or how it turns its head as it flies, may be all it takes to *know*.[25] Blink!: a powerful impression is gained that cannot necessarily be described in words.

JURY THINKING

ALL OF US ARE OLD HANDS AT THIN-SLICING THE WORLD AROUND US AND PRODUCING RAPID IMPRESSIONS OF VALUE.

What we are not used to, however, is accounting for the fact that each juror is blinking, from the moment that juror enters the courtroom.

§ 2-1(d). Issue-Specific Blink

Researchers have begun to look more closely at the way snap judgments, beneath the level of conscious thinking, affect our beliefs and judgments. A number of psychologists from universities across the country have cooperated in designing an implicit association interactive test (IAT),[26] based upon a simple but significant observation:

> PEOPLE MAKE CONNECTIONS MORE QUICKLY BETWEEN PAIRS OF IDEAS THAT ARE **ALREADY RELATED** IN THEIR MINDS THAN THEY DO BETWEEN PAIRS OF IDEAS THAT ARE **UNFAMILIAR** TO THEM.

One of the most practical things you might do to revise and enrich your trial skills would be to join in that study, now available to anyone, on the Harvard University Web site at: www.implicit.harvard.edu.

Practice Tip: Take the Implicit Association Test

- First, notice on the web site that you have a choice. You can directly participate in the study, which involves a wide variety of variables, and which will profoundly inform the way you understand yourself as a judge, attorney, consultant, or human being. You can choose to participate in the "demonstration." Go for the full study; this is too important to miss and will change the way you talk to and select jurors in every trial.

- Second, encourage people you know to take the test and share their results with you. Finding out the surprising effects of implicit associations that firmly dwell in the brains of people we thought we knew is enormously enlightening.

- Consider encouraging your staff, associates, investigators, interns, students, and experts to take the IAT test on the web. You will all grow enormously from the experience, but, further, will now develop a shared vocabulary, based on the test itself and the personal insights gained. Any works-together group of people (however small in num-

> ber) functions more effectively and compassionately when members *think about* their own BLINK! snap judgments.

The IAT test itself offers categories vulnerable to snap judgments in jurors (implicit associations) that arise in many trials: weight (fat/thin), weapons, disability, age (young/old), religion, gender, skin tone, race, sexuality (gay/straight). Malcolm Gladwell[27] discusses the fact that he has taken the Race IAT on many occasions and the results always leave him feeling a bit creepy:

> I think of the races as equal. Then comes the test. You're encouraged to complete it quickly. First comes the warm-up. A series of pictures of faces flash on the screen. When you see a black face, you press *e* and put it in the left-hand category. When you see a white face, you press *I* and put it in the right-hand category. It's *blink, blink, blink*: I didn't have to think at all. Then comes part one. Flash choices . . . Immediately, something strange happened to me. The task of putting the words and faces in the right categories suddenly became more difficult. I found myself slowing down. I had to think. Sometimes I assigned something to one category when I really meant to assign it to the other category. I was trying as hard as I could, and in the back of my mind was a growing sense of mortification. Why was I having such trouble when I had to put a word like "Glorious" or "Wonderful" into the "Good" category when "Good" was paired with "African American" or when I had to put the word "Evil" into the "Bad" Category when "Bad" was paired with "European American"? . . . I took the test a second time, and then a third time, and then a fourth time, hoping that the awful feeling of bias would go away. It made no difference. It turns out that more than 80 percent of all those who have ever taken the test end up having pro-white associations, meaning that it takes them measurably longer to complete answers when they are required to put good words into the "Black" category than when they are required to link bad things with black people.

Then the author described the most startling aspect of his test:

> I didn't do quite so badly. On the Race IAT, I was rated as having a "moderate automatic preference for whites." But then again, I'm half black.[28]

Our attitudes toward things like race, gender, skin tone, disability, age, or religion operate on *two levels*: **conscious** attitudes (what we choose to believe and how we choose to describe ourselves) and our **unconscious** attitudes (immediate blink associations that tumble out before we think). The IAT doesn't just abstractly measure attitudes, but is a powerful *predictor* of how people will act or react in a spontaneous unfamiliar situation. **Implicit association blink** has powerful explanatory power for why our clients or various witnesses behaved the way they did, *even though they will never be aware of the cause*, because they do not know their own minds.

Practice Tip: Explain the unexplainable unthinking blink and help folks chew on it.

- *Jurors.* Develop voir dire on implicit association blink and see which jurors make room for the possibility that it has affected them, and which jurors reject that possibility.

- *Other People.* Ask jurors for examples of how they have seen *implicit association blink* [after you explain it] affect people, even though they did not realize or admit it.

- *Other Jurors.* Help jurors anticipate the implicit associations that may creep into deliberations by discussing it during closing and offering ways to untangle it or call it for what it is.

For proof that *you can combat juror prejudice*, read the more recent studies on the malleability of automatic attitudes, particularly those using images of admired and disliked individuals or the use of imagining stereotypes away.[29]

§ 2-1(e). Blink and Voir Dire

Jury selection has long been experienced by trial attorneys as a cruel form of **speed-dating**,[4] where too little time is offered to talk to too many people in order to make quick decisions about who to invite on the trial date. Undoubtedly, citizens called for jury duty have similar experiences: they report that they were confused about why they were kept, or worried about why they were excused, or upset about why they were not talked to in greater length. As if it were a form of *speed-dating*, sometimes the attraction between attorney and potential juror may not have been mutual. Jurors, at least, get immediate feedback (excused or

---

4. Speed-dating is a new ritual, based on *blink snap judgments*: in a large room singles are paired off, with five minutes to talk to one another. When the bell rings, they must move on to the next person, after filling out a quick form. If they like someone after 5 minutes they check a box; later, when tallied, only mutually-selected people are given email addresses. The atmosphere is full of anticipation and strained small talk, all designed to answer the question: *Do I want to see this person again?* It turns out that people don't need an entire evening to *know*. One dater explained, "He lost me at hello." Not unlike jury selection.

accepted), while attorneys may not realize they were *not selected* until the verdict is announced.

§ 2-2. Mental Leaps

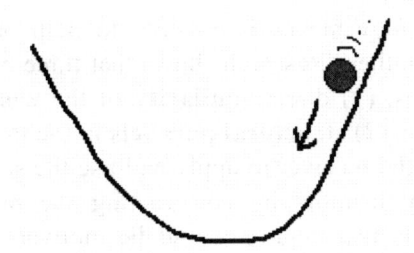

Every trial demands that each juror successfully complete thousands of mental leaps. It is comforting to imagine that we see the world the way it actually is. In fact, however, our conceptions of the world are largely our personal mental creations, so our confident sense of directly understanding the world is a robust illusion (see, "How a Juror Becomes Aware of a 'Fact,'" § 2-2, and Memory, § 3-2, PRACTICAL JURY DYNAMICS).[30] The brain **re-imagines** the experiences and behaviors of other people, even as it first receives images and attempts to name them. Consequently, *images* become powerful communication tools for helping jurors immediately "imagine" significant events in a trial. Images help a juror's brain to make the **mental leap** from *someone else's past experience* to the juror's present understanding of that experience.

Among the language tools that can help a juror with some of the mental leaps that the trial task demands is **analogy**. *Analogy* is a mental tool that is well-developed in children, who naturally have fewer experiences than adults upon which to draw comparisons as they encounter new experiences or information. Consequently, children will attempt to understand new experiences by creating their own analogies ("That tree has arms and the tree is waving at me!").

We have not paid sufficient attention to the manner in which a juror, who encounters the need to make a mental leap in the courtroom, may engage in analogical thinking (whether or not the lawyers choose to participate in the creation of analogy). A **source analogy** comes from the familiar (people have arms) and what someone already understands. A **target analogy** is a relatively unfamiliar domain that someone (a juror) is trying to understand. *Analogical thinking* helps make the mental leap, but this type of thinking is not logical in the sense of thoughtful reflection; rather it is more like *blink-thinking*.

§ 2-2(a). Expanding a Juror's Internal Thinking Criteria

> Consciousness is the great poem of matter. But consciousness isn't really a response to the world, it's more of an opinion about it.
>
> —Diane Ackerman, *An Alchemy of Mind*[31]

What about an *analogy* makes it possible to help people understand one situation in terms of another? Research shows that three basic factors characterize successful analogies: (1) direct **similarity** of the elements involved in the target and source image, (2) **structural parallels** in the target and source image, and (3) **motivation** in the receiver to apply and use the suggested analogy. As a result, a trial attorney benefits by constructing the most similar analogies possible for trial events that a juror would be motivated to understand more clearly. Even to propose an analogy to someone else requires taking a kind of mental leap.

Fortunately for trial lawyers, however, analogies are recognized as *a source of potential (or plausible) conjectures,* not irrefutable conclusions.

Practice Tip: Anticipate analogy-rebuttal.

When offering an analogy to the jury, anticipate that your opponent may, at some point, point out the difference. At the time you offer an analogy, point out that analogies are tools and are never meant to be exactly the same; offer examples from everyday life that show jurors how useful an analogy is to get us thinking in new useful ways. Empower the jurors by reminding them that everyone is different and that an analogy may be useful to get one juror thinking, while another juror does not find it useful.

By understanding how the human mind naturally thinks in analogy, you can hope to put the tool to good use in persuading jurors. Remember (remind jurors, as well) that analogy has many guises, all involving useful but indirect communication: parables, fables, myths, and metaphors. It turns out that there is something inherently pleasurable about finding a mesh between two situations that seemed superficially unrelated.[32]

Remind yourself (and jurors) that the fundamental purpose of analogy is to help us gain understanding that goes beyond the information we receive from our senses. Jurors who are teachers, religious leaders, or health care practitioners may be able to share useful examples of how they use analogy to explain new concepts to students, parishioners, or patients.

§ 2-2(b). Creating Successful Mental Leaps

Once two situations have been associated in a suggested analogy, it needs to be pre-tested for coherency, as well as inferences that may not have been immediately obvious to the analogy creator. Despite the intuitive appeal of an analogy created by a lawyer, inferences generated by that analogy can turn out to be wrong, seriously incomplete, or distorted in the minds of some people. Mental leaping with analogies, as a result, can benefit from focus group work, either formally or informally.

Do not seek to understand whether an analogy is successful or fails. Instead, present it pre-trial with the goal of understanding *for whom it succeeded* and, at the same time, *for whom it failed*. Both results may surprise you and the focus event can be as traditional, formal, or casual as you choose. Both attorneys and judges should rethink, for example, the analogies they have been tirelessly using to explain legal principles. Besides lacking freshness and today-relevancy, it turns out that many jurors do not connect with them (i.e., reasonable doubt is wondering if you forgot to unplug the iron, if you hesitated at all, you had reasonable doubt; the burden of proof is like cooking spaghetti, if you leave out the oregano, it is not spaghetti; opening statements are like road maps to help you understand a complex puzzle). Consider the cost of making a mistake based on the demonstrated value of the analogy to a variety of real people today.

Analogies should enhance thinking, not substitute for it. When helping jurors think about an opponent's offered analogy, there are three attacks available:

Practice Tip: Help jurors attack analogies.

Remind jurors in closing argument that an analogy must be evaluated. Every analogy offered can yield one of three verdicts in a juror's mind: (1) the "source" can usefully be applied in thinking about the new "target," or (2) the "source" should not be applied to the target because they are significantly different, or (3) the "source" offered [analogy] can be applied to the target *with modifications*.

Chapter 3

RE-THINKING

I screamed that I couldn't believe this was happening, that we were possibly going to be a hung jury when in my mind the case was so obvious. Everything was there, DNA evidence, witness testimony. There was no room for interpretation. I was angry. There were words of profanity that came out of my mouth.

Juror describing the fifth day of deliberations (2004)

The Decision is not the problem. The Outcome is the problem.

— Zen teaching

Decisional tasks are not generally welcomed, since decisions involving complex choices with many imagined outcomes. It stands to reason, therefore, that the more important the perceived outcome of any trial, the greater the dislike a juror will have of facing that decision. Re-thinking happens.

§ 3-1. Juror Flipping

> The air reeked of hatred and people were angry and I had never been in an atmosphere like that before.
>
> 79-year-old juror,
> describing her regretted verdict in the Michael Jackson trial
> (August 2005)

Most jurors re-think their intended votes *during* deliberations—such re-thinking is one of the valued opportunities that shared deliberative time is designed to provide. Some jurors, however, re-think their actual votes *after* deliberations have concluded—a situation that our legal system is not designed to accommodate. Some trials are more likely to produce **jury flipping** (re-thinking) than others.

Three principles of juror re-thinking are worth paying attention to:

- A VERDICT IS MORE LIKELY TO BE REGRETTED BY A JUROR WHEN THE VERDICT'S CONSEQUENCES ARE PERCEIVED AS BEING BOTH HIGHLY *SALIENT* AND *PUBLIC*.

- INDIVIDUAL JUROR VERDICTS (VOTES) ARE MORE LIKELY TO BE SURRENDERED DURING DELIBERATIONS WHEN THE TRIAL HAS BEEN *LENGTHY* AND A JUROR THINKS THAT A *HUNG JURY* WOULD RESULT WITHOUT A VOTE CHANGE.

- A SURRENDERED JUROR VOTE DURING DELIBERATIONS (IN A TRIAL THAT WAS BOTH HIGHLY SALIENT AND PUBLIC) IS LIKELY TO BE REGRETTED BY THE SURRENDERING JUROR(S) LATER.

The process of consciously re-thinking personal votes during deliberative discussion is never an easy juror task. Further, the group's deliberative *culture* that helped produce a vote-surrender will dissolve after the jury is discharged—leaving some jurors confused in the aftermath about why they did not stick to their initial vote. Any **jury's communication culture** may have included unspoken talking "rules" and styles to which some jurors were either sensitive or unfamiliar: yelling, rapid talk, simultaneous talk, interruptions, tears, teasing, bullying, name-calling, or threats, to name a few [rules and norms of deliberation introduced in § 10-1 and § 10-2, PRACTICAL JURY DYNAMICS]. Some jurors experience deliberative argument as **toxic talk**—it makes them emotionally or physically ill, stressed, or anxious; the juror can *exit* the toxic situation by re-thinking their position [see § 13-4, toxic jurors, and § 13-1, grouphate, PRACTICAL JURY DYNAMICS].

Anticipated deadlock triggers re-thinking. Notwithstanding judicial instructions or attorney explanations, most jurors think that their service has been "wasted" if the jurors deadlock. *Agreeing to disagree* is not thought of as one type of *judicial success*. It follows that the more time that jurors have invested in a trial, the harder it will be for some jurors to tolerate a hung jury (whether they are in the majority or minority).

A vivid example **of juror-verdict-regret** emerged as this book went to press: After more than 130 witnesses and almost five months of trial, a jury of eight women and four men in California found entertainer-defendant Michael Jackson not guilty of all criminal charges. Their deliberations had lasted more than seven days (32 hours). Two months later, on August 8, 2005, two of those jurors (one man, one woman) claimed on national television that they personally believed Michael Jackson to have been guilty and, further, that they regretted their not guilty verdicts.[33] While one juror explained that he could not tolerate the idea of a hung jury (necessitating a retrial), after all the time he had put into the trial, the second juror tearfully blamed group dynamics and a threat she received from the foreperson:

> He said if I could not change my mind or go with the group or be more understanding, that he would have to notify the bailiff, the bailiff would notify the judge, and the judge would have me removed.

The physical anxiety produced by group argument after a lengthy trial was real for this juror, as she then described her heart palpitating and the "gut wrenching" position she felt she was in with other jurors. She began to mentally *reframe* her position for herself as perhaps "ambivalent," in order, she explained, "to stop the pain."

Trial attorneys and judges have largely ignored the unwanted effects of the **biology of disagreement** or the **biology of argument** that can emerge for some jurors during deliberations [see above, § 1-1, The Biology of Beliefs; also § 5-7 through § 5-9, the effects of stress and anxiety on jurors, PRACTICAL JURY DYNAMICS]. Two salient times to bring up the issue of painful arguments are during jury selection (with the goal of identifying or eliminating jurors who are toxic or who might be intolerant of a highly charged argument atmospheres) or, later, at the close of the trial, when judges or attorneys can offer all jurors predeliberative remedies (with the goal of reducing toxic stress during deliberations, reporting it, or healing it so that individual votes are not affected).

> **Practice Tip:** For trial lawyers, the critical issue is to discover whether a juror who is either (a) **toxic** or (b) **allergic** can be anticipated to be a juror *in favor of your client's position*. Potential bully or victim? Prior experiences with group argument are most useful in the search.
>
> **Voir Dire:** We were all raised in families with different styles of argument, some loud, some quiet, some explosive. Can you describe the style of argument you are most used to? [Answer.] Is there a style of argument that bothers you a little? [Answer.] Can you give an example?
>
> **Voir Dire:** Some people have no problem with others who yell to get their point across, but that bothers some of us. Where do you stand? [Answer.] Why?
>
> **Voir Dire:** There's something that might affect your vote and I'd like to ask you about that. What if you are in deliberations and a couple of the jurors start raising their voices, maybe even yelling. Are you a just-ignore-it person, join-in-and-get-your-point-across person, or a person who finds that a little offensive?
>
> **Voir Dire:** A lot of jurors have honestly told us that arguing in a small room with people they don't really know gives them a headache. What do you think? Can that happen for a normal person?
>
> **Voir Dire:** What is the best way, in your opinion, for a group to handle an intensive argument? Can you give an example?
>
> **Questionnaire:** How often do you get headaches? Do you take any medications for anxiety or stress? How often have you been in a professional group that argued in making a decision? What groups have you been in that argued and yelled at times?

> **Practice Tip:** Judges want to insure a fair verdict, as well as satisfactory jury service for individual jurors. Prophylactic coaching on group argument can help jurors before it gets painful:
>
> YOU ARE INSTRUCTED THAT YOUR DISCUSSIONS SHOULD BE A FAIR SHARING OF IDEAS AND LISTENING TO OPINIONS. ALL JURORS SHOULD HELP INSURE THAT NO YELLING, INTERRUPTING, BULLYING,

> THREATENING, OR SCOLDING OF ANY JUROR OCCURS. IF IT DOES, REPORT IT TO ME PRIVATELY IN A NOTE AND I WILL HELP GET THINGS BACK ON TRACK.
>
> - Attorneys can request such an instruction be given.
>
> - In closing arguments, it is important to request that the jurors pay attention to the process of talking to one another, sharing turns, and protecting one another. If the process is not fair to any juror, the verdict may not reflect justice. Attorneys can give jurors a "heads up" on dysfunctional arguments, tools to get past that, or, again, suggest that when deliberations become unpleasant for any juror that all jurors have a duty to report that fact and trust the trial judge to help them.

There is another compelling explanation for the recent Michael Jackson trial **juror-regret** phenomena, which points out that this sort of thing can be anticipated as a normal part of juror thinking. One line of research describing mental processes *after* a decision has been made has pointed out that people often experience *post*decisional dissonance.[34] Further complicating the decision-making challenge, immediately after making a decision people have a tendency to focus on the negative aspects about the choice made, as well as the positive aspects of the choice rejected. In order to reduce dissonance and feel better about a decision, people may enhance the attractiveness of the chosen alternative, while devaluing the rejected alternatives. As a result, a juror who was ambivalent before the verdict decision can be expected to experience post-verdict thinking that enhances the reasons the verdict was wrong and that the other verdict would have been wiser.

> **Practice Tip**: Normalize and anticipate Verdict Regret with jurors.
>
> - Ask jurors during jury selection if they have ever experienced intense decisional regret. *Collaborate* (How can we minimize that in a trial?) or *Harvest* (Tell me how often that happens? What has that been like for you?)
>
> - Discuss the issue during closing in a way that will help your jurors recognize decisional regret and avoid it in your favor. Discuss the issue during closing in a way that will help your jurors recognize that decisional regret may be blocking other jurors from joining them and point them in a useful direction.

"Your Honor, on the first ballot the jury voted ten to two for conviction. For three emotionally charged hours, we discussed our points of difference. On the next ballot, it was seven to five for acquittal. Over the next several ballots, the vote seesawed back and forth. One juror became ill and was replaced by an alternate. By now, we had been in session for ten hours straight. Tempers were rising and some jurors were near the breaking point."

© The New Yorker Collection 1986 Dana Fradon from cartoonbank.com. All Rights Reserved.

§ 3-2. Ignoring Regret

A new study (scheduled to be published in January 2006, Northwestern Law Review) is causing judges, court reformers, and scholars to pause in their assumptions about the fairness of jury deliberations. **Nonunanimous juries** operate in the majority of states across the country in civil trials. Nonunanimous juries were designed, in part, to reduce the number of hung juries—by preventing "obstinate" jurors from deadlocking deliberations. Opponents of rules that permit some numerical majority of jurors to render a verdict have argued that dissent is suppressed and the evidence, as a result, is not rigorously tested by the jurors. The findings from this new study supports that concern.

It appears that when nonunanimous rule juries reach a perceived consensus, they frequently just dismiss dissenting views, silencing their contributions to critical thinking about the evidence or law. The video tapes of trials of various types, lengths, and complexities were made in Arizona from 1998 to 2001 to evaluate the innovations recently made that allowed jurors to become more active in trials. Many of the juries in this study took votes at the outset, before discussing the evidence at all, then cut off debate if they realized they had the numbers to reach a verdict, by-passing deliberations entirely.

For dissenting jurors who were not in the majority, regret was experienced, then quickly by-passed. **By-passed regret** taints the deliberative process. Former dissenters explained later that at the last moment they would side with the majority, bowing to the inevitable and reluctant to attempt what appeared to be an impossible task of persuasion within the group. The researchers concluded that a thoughtful minority of jurors may, in fact, be marginalized when majority jurors have the power to ignore them in reaching a verdict. Surprisingly, the study also reports that trial judges would have sided with dissenting jurors in six of the 13 nonunanimous trials; there was no evidence that the dissenting jurors' positions were either odd or extreme. Further, there was no evidence that the dissenting jurors were more likely to favor the plaintiff or defendant.

> **Practice Tip**: Instruct the jurors on the role of dissenting jurors in nonunanimous rule juries.
>
> - While judges can instruct, *sua sponte*, advocates also have the choice of either drafting and requesting an instruction, or discussion the role of dissent during closing arguments, when it will be highly salient to the jury pre-deliberation.
> - In cases that are bifurcated (liability, then damages), instruct the jury on the role dissenters to the liability portion of the verdict are allowed to play in the damages deliberative discussions on damages.

Jurors are often aware of the dysfunctional effects on their deliberations of nonunanimous verdict rules. In this study, jurors in the nonunanimous juries rated their deliberations as *less thorough* and their fellow jurors as *less open-minded* than did the jurors who were on unanimous verdict juries.

Deliberations are intended to offer a safeguard against error, with *listening* to one another before deciding a primary goal. Instead, when conflict is suppressed and discussion/listening turns are confined to those who agree, the deliberative process is subverted—particularly in lengthy or complex trials where some members of the jury already suffer from stress, anxiety, and information overload. Importantly, **tentative votes** may be offered that will be perceived by other jurors as firm votes, which can influence both the perception of consensus or the perception of the uselessness of dissenting to other jurors.

Practice Tip: Warn the jury about **premature verdict closure**.

- **Closing Argument:** Sometimes a jury is so anxious for agreement, that some jurors falsely conclude that a proper consensus has been reached. Every juror helps the group by speaking up and suggesting that a more thorough discussion is needed.

- **Closing Argument:** Sometimes a juror offers a *tentative* vote because an early vote was requested. When you vote, but feel tentative, because a full discussion has not yet occurred, it gives the wrong signals to other jurors. You might want to have the rule, "We don't vote when some of us are still tentative." Calling for a vote early can hurt the speaking and listening deliberations were designed to offer.

- **Closing Argument:** By the way, as you are discussing these things, remember that the way the jury deliberates must be fully just for the verdict to be just. No juror should be asked to vote before they have a firm verdict in their heart and mind. No juror should agree to a vote when they are not yet fully certain of their own verdict on any issue.

---

§ 3-3. If-Only Thinking

I've never looked at the consequences of missing a big shot. When you think about the consequences, you always think of a negative result.

—Michael Jordan

I see it all perfectly. There are two possible situations—one can either do this or that. My honest opinion and my friendly advice is this: Do it or do not do it. You will regret both.

—Soren Kierkegaard (Danish philosopher, 1813-1855)

There exists a compelling intuition that the anticipation of regret is a significant factor in decision making.[35] Highly salient possible verdict outcomes generate anxiety for jurors during decisional talk and affect their personal thinking. A juror may wonder how a verdict choice might affect the parties, the attorneys, the judge, their community, the press, outsiders, and, perhaps, their families. Other jurors may "catch" the anxiety. **Regret contagion**, in which one group member's regret anxiety may be transferred to other group members, can be triggered by the communication of counterfactual narratives during decisional talk.

So common is decisional regret in juries that it can be anticipated in all trials with highly salient outcomes, with significant publicity, or that are lengthy in time. **Decisional Regret Theory** explains the manner in which regret arises in the jury room, touching first an individual juror's thinking as that juror approaches choosing a personal vote.[36] One of the most interesting understandings about jury thinking to emerge from Decisional Regret Theory is the fact that when the verdict decision is painful, some jurors will engage in a type of thinking involving **re-storying the trial**.

Jurors begin to imagine what *could have happened* so that there couldn't even *be* a trial! This is **counterfactual thinking**. One effect of such re-storying ("If only he'd called someone first!") during decisional talk may involve simply delaying the decisional task. Group members may think about an outcome that would have been *better* than what actually occurred *if only someone had behaved differently* (no child abuse, no breach, no surgery, no contract, no shooting, to name a few).

Counterfactual thinking is common in dog mauling and medical malpractice, cases, for example, because jurors prefer to imagine the tragedies being avoided. *Such stories offer a fantasized reality, in which decision makers imagine that they would never have to be faced with the current decision at all.* If the story of how someone should have behaved differently than they did is joined or re-storied by others, the jury may be diverted from its painful decisional task. As a result, this form of jury thinking must be anticipated by trial lawyers. [See extensive discussion of "what might have been" thinking in PRACTICAL JURY DYNAMICS, § 14-2 and § 14-3.]

Decisional regret and a juror's inclination to re-story the trial in a way that would have avoided the trauma, injuries, or lawsuit can be usefully anticipated.

JURY THINKING

> **Practice Tip: Maximize or neutralize counterfactual thinking.**
>
> - When the damages could easily be imagined to have been avoidable by a juror, both plaintiffs and prosecutors may be benefitted, since a juror can think about the many ways the defendant could have behaved differently, notwithstanding the legal principles. Avoiding terrible damages is a thought coupled with powerful emotions, so the longer and more vivid the list generated by an attorney during closing of all the things within a defendant's control or choice that could have been avoided, the more likely a juror will engage in counterfactual thinking along those lines during deliberations.
>
> - Defendants must strategize knowing how normal it will be for jurors to think this way, even if their opponent does not suggest it. This involves counterfactual arguments in closing. These arguments suggest to the jurors what to say if (a) they start thinking that way or (b) another juror starts arguing the point. Neutralize thoughts about *undoing what already happened* by: bringing the jurors back to the law, reminding them of the many variables at the doors of other people involved, and letting them know how natural it is to think that way even though that cannot be part of the trial. Examples of how that will always take us back to someone's cradle can be useful, using humor.

> From now on, I'll connect the dots my own way.
>
> —Calvin (Calvin & Hobbes)

§ 3-4. Binge-Think

> **binge**, *n.*, a spree of excessive indulgence in some activity; *v.i.*, to do or consume something in an unrestrained, self-indulgent way

Do you binge-think?

Probably. Jurors do, too. When does **binge-thinking** occur and how might binge-thinking affect a juror's trial task?[37]

RE-THINKING

The essence of **juror binge-think**[5] at trial is ***unproductive over-thinking***. Hence, *juror binge-think* has three attributes that make it worth paying attention to:

Excessive

Uncontrolled

Toxic

Juror binge-think involves a type of thinking that is unwanted at trial. By virtue of it being a **binge**, there's too much of it, it runs out-of-control, and its effects are toxic to the decision-making task. At the outset, consider a comparison of juror binge-think to alcohol binge-drink:[6]

Binge Drinking	Binge Thinking
Voluntary indulgence in excessive behavior occurs (for an activity that is acceptable when done in moderation).	Voluntary indulgence in excessive behavior occurs (for an activity that is acceptable when done in moderation).
Drinker loses control of the behavior.	Thinker loses control of the behavior.
May be performed privately (drinking alone)	May be performed privately (thinking).
When performed publicly, it is often reinforced and encouraged by others.	When performed publicly, it is often reinforced and encouraged by others.
The behavior may be done by only one, or, by several members of a group.	The behavior may be done by only one, or, by several members of a group.

---

5. "Juror binge-think" is a concept introduced for the first time here. "Group binge-thinking" is suggested as an additional concept that offers a useful new lens through which to view and understand some of the dynamics of group decision making in other contexts.

6. There are other forms of binging, of course, including eating, shopping, hoarding, or gambling, to name a few.

Binge Drinking	Binge Thinking
The behavior is toxic to the drinker's brain.	The behavior is toxic to the thinker's brain.
The behavior travels in a downward out-of-control spiral that could be (but generally is not) stopped by the group watching it.	The behavior travels in a downward out-of-control spiral that could be (but generally is not) stopped by the group watching it.
There is a risk of death to the drinker.	There is a risk of killing a group's task.
A painful hangover to the brain results.	A painful hangover to the brain results.
Episode amnesia: later, the drinker may not remember what they did.	Episode amnesia: later, the thinker may not remember what they said or thought.
People know that binge drinking is risky behavior.	People may be unaware that binge thinking is risky behavior.

Binge-*drinking* has devastating effects on both public health and society (in our communities). **Binge-thinking** can have devastating *effects on the health of a trial* and the *community of jurors* chosen to decide the issues.

Like binge-drinking, **socially-shared binge-thinking** has become *fashionable* in some circles, deemed an acceptable form of personal **thought purging** for special occasions. Self-help therapy. Like binge-drinking, binge-thinking is performed both privately (addiction) as well as *publicly* (social acceptance).

WHAT JURORS PROBABLY DO NOT REALIZE IS THAT BINGE-THINKING

(BY ANY ONE OF THEM) CAN BE DANGEROUS TO A JUST VERDICT.

§ 3-4(a). Juror Thinking Binges

When can we expect juror thinking binges? Juror binge-thinking can occur in any trial, but it is can be expected to occur in a trial when *several* of the following variables exist:

RE-THINKING

- MULTIPLE ISSUES ARE PRESENT
- THE TRIAL WAS LENGTHY
- MEDIA COVERAGE HAS BEEN EXTENSIVE
- MAJOR HARM TO SOMEONE HAS ALREADY OCCURRED
- MULTIPLE ACTS OF WRONGDOING BY DIFFERENT PEOPLE HAVE OCCURRED
- COMPLEX LEGAL INSTRUCTIONS
- MULTIPLE VERDICTS ARE REQUIRED
- THE VERDICT WILL HAVE MAJOR IMPACT ON OTHERS

The above variables may trigger intense ruminations (**deep thinking**) by some jurors. Deep thinking is a good thing—deep thinking, however, stands on the dangerous edge of the binge-thinking precipice.

WHEN A JUROR IS STRESSED BY THE COMPLEXITY OF THE TASK OR THE MAGNITUDE OF THE VERDICT-OUTCOME, THE CONDITIONS FOR BINGE-THINKING TO THRIVE HAVE BEEN FURNISHED.

A rich example of juror binge-thinking in a real world jury is available on video-tape. In 1986 the television program *Frontline* was given permission to film a criminal trial, as well as the deliberations of the jurors.[38] In that case the charge involved simply "felon in possession of a weapon," generally regarded as a slam-dunk for a prosecutor. The defense was further blocked from arguing "jury nullification"; although that state allowed jury nullification as a verdict, the trial judge ruled that the defense attorney could not argue or explain jury nullification to the jurors during closing. The trial judge acknowledged that the jurors could *do* nullification, but ruled that no one could tell them about that possibility.

At the outset of the deliberations in this trial, one of the jurors described the difficulty she felt in thinking about her verdict and, then, she reframed the jury's task as, "What is a jury?" This juror was a school psychologist, so this rumination was comfortable for her.

The deliberating jurors were subsequently split into two camps: (1) those who felt the jury's task was to determine whether the elements of the charge had been proven beyond a reasonable doubt, and (2) those who felt that something more important and complex was involved, "What is a jury?"

The resulting discussion was painful for many of them, bringing tears into what is not generally considered by lawyers to be a tearful issue. *While binge-thinking may be in the eye or ear of the beholder*, it can be argued that rich binge-thinking occurred in the subsequent deliberations of these jurors. One juror attempted to stop that thinking, complaining in bewilderment, "I think some of you are going way too much into this thing. I think if I held up this pencil, some of you would say, 'Well, is that *really* a pencil?'"

Binge-thinking is painful to listen to, but it is not always clear to the group how to stop it. Juror binge-thinking, when shared during deliberations with the other jurors, may also be **contagious** (see, emotional contagion in Chapter 12, emotional deliberations, & Chapter 14, decisional regrets in the jury room, PRACTICAL JURY DYNAMICS), as it was for many of these jurors, after the school psychologist shared her thinking. While some jurors may decide to join and reinforce **shared binge-thinking**, others may feel blocked and frustrated in the verdict task. Deadlock is a real threat at this point.

In the video jury, after deeply-shared emotions, one juror finally said that he did not agree with the group, felt frustrated, thought they were completely off their proper task, told them they were analyzing it too much, but he was going to change his vote to go along with them, "But I will *never* feel right about it!"

The proper verdict in many trials may be an agreement-to-disagree. On the other hand, an agreed verdict is never a just verdict if a juror has simply given up and feels overwhelmed by the complex philosophical thinking of other jurors. **Shared deliberative analysis** that is felt to be *extreme* by some jurors is problematic, but has rarely been discussed by trial advocates. In large part, this is because we have had, to date, only limited access to watch and listen to real world jury deliberations.

Once you have watched a jury video and seen real deliberative communication that reeks of *binge-thinking* by one or more jurors, it becomes clear **that either judicial instructions or closing arguments shoulda/coulda address possible binge-thinking before it happens.**

It should be noted here, further, that binge-thinking by jurors will not show up in mock trials because the above listed triggers will not be present. Participants know that there will be no real world consequences to their verdicts, that they have been reading a transcript or watching actors, and there is no media coverage or complex issues. *Binge-thinking is one more excellent reason to encourage more research on real world jury thinking outside the laboratory* (§ 1-3(b), criticism of jury studies, PRACTICAL JURY DYNAMICS). It is also possible that <u>one party may benefit from binge-thinking in jury deliberations</u>, which heightens the reasons for both parties to anticipate the issue.

§ 3-4(b).   The Binge-Think Hangover

The binge **hangover** shows up after the deliberative party. It is accompanied by "holes" in thinking (episodic amnesia), in which the hungover juror may not accurately remember what was said during deliberations when recalling them later.

Painful **juror regret** (discussed earlier in this chapter) is one *symptom* of a binge-think hangover from deliberations. In fact, in lengthy media-covered trials, there may be a familiar path that the **binge-think hangover** takes for some jurors:

> deep thinking during deliberations ➔ thinking not reinforced by other jurors ➔ juror flipping to agree with majority ➔ post-verdict ruminations ➔ regret ➔ interviews ➔ books ➔ more ruminations and criticism ➔ regret

An unfortunate outcome of a *binge-think hangover* may be a mutual cycle of criticism between jurors (evidenced in the example of the Michael Jackson trial jurors). A hungover juror criticizes the other jurors, followed by various jurors criticizing the juror who is now expressing regret. Media, attorneys, court personal, parties, and witnesses may join in the free-flowing post-verdict criticisms. These criticisms are comparable to the social criticisms commonly leveled at those who were present during a binge-drinking episode of someone else:

> Why didn't you stop it?
>
> Why didn't you recognize it had gone too far?
>
> Why didn't you bring him home safely?

No one should be driving after binge-*drinking*.

IT MAY BE THAT JURORS SHOULD NOT BE VOTING AFTER AN INTENSE EPISODE OF BINGE-THINKING.

Binge-think affects everyone differently. It never feels good afterwards. **Sobering up is needed first.** A juror alert to this in advance can request it or suggest it if the issue appears to emerge.

We can help jurors recognize the binge-thinking of fellow jurors during deliberations and suggest ways to help *bring them all home safely.*[39]

§ 3-4(c). The Binge-Think Intervention

If binge-thinking occurs during deliberation, what should jurors do?

Binge-think is a particularly useful concept to talk to jurors about at the outset of certain trials. It may usefully stimulate a juror's **Metaphoric Thinking** (Chapter 4, below). Many jurors, outside of court, have been crusaders for campaigns to curb drinking and driving and will readily attach to the binge-think metaphor (as well as remember it during deliberations). Painful *binge-thinking* can also be the outcome for a juror who is unsuccessfully attempting to cope with thinking about an **unavoidable paradox** (Chapter 6, below), as a result of specific trial issues.

> **Practice Tip: Make a juror an active participant in *the life of their own mind*.**
>
> During closing argument, it is helpful to guide jurors into the pathways their deliberations might take and to point out, as a guide, the thinking of their fellow jurors that they might encounter on the journey. Their own thoughts may not be honored and their own thoughts may feel chaotic. Rather than give up on their own deep thinking, motivate them. Suggest to jurors:
>
> Notice your thoughts during deliberations. Get the help you need to decrease ineffective thinking and increase productive thinking:
>
> *Stand up!*
>
> *Ask questions!*
>
> *Make your own decision.*
>
> If you need silence, ask for it. If you need a break, others will honor it. If you need to ask the judge a question, just do it!

> **Practice Tip: Thinking about Thinking about a Thing Too Much.**
>
> It is valuable to have language to offer to a juror about a topic that can quickly get uncomfortably slippery. **Binge-thinking** does that. Give that confusion a name. Ask jurors if they have seen it in other people (friends, co-workers, relatives).
>
> - On questionnaires you can ask about the longest they ever spent thinking about an important decision,
>
> - about any rules they have about how long someone should think about an important decision,
>
> - and about what their own opinion is about over-thinking something.
>
> - Have them give examples.
>
> These questions offer a wonderful window into the type of thinking potential jurors may bring to a case during deliberations. It further gets them thinking about *their own wonderful minds* (before they have to dust them off, oil them up, calibrate them, and engage them in the unfamiliar trial task).

Consequently, judges and attorneys should make a commitment to promoting the positive benefits of moderation in intense thinking, which can reduce the risk of tainted votes, task exhaustion, or deadlock.

Chapter 4

SYMBOLIC THINKING

Language ties a string between a word and the thing it stands for.

—Bart Kosko, *Fuzzy Thinking*, p. 5

§ 4-1. God Words and Devil Words

Jury thinking invites us to pay attention to the persuasive use of words. Some words are better than others at getting our point across to jurors in a vivid way—that will be retained, remembered, and recalled at a later point in time. Since we rely heavily on the power of words to persuade, we can draw from the experience of advertisers. Marketing scholars and practitioners have long understood the power of two particular types of words that affect the way a juror thinks:

GOD WORDS

DEVIL WORDS

Intriguingly, these words are hardly noticed in everyday life, but they stand out in a listener's processing mind. In fact, they stand out so much they seem to have a special power. The advocate who knows these words and how to use them wields persuasive power.

> A WORD IS A GOD WORD OR A DEVIL WORD IF, BY ITSELF,
> THAT WORD EVOKES A POWERFUL EMOTION FOR MOST PEOPLE.

God Words are rebuked at the attacker's peril: you cannot argue against the value of motherhood or patriotism, for example. Such words often capsulate beliefs, attitudes, or values. In a way, everyday use and community values have canonized some words, making them unchallengeable. Communities, however, vary: a medical community, or religious community, for-profit organization, or farming community have canonized quite different words. The argument that something is *profitable* invokes a God Word in a profit-making organization and makes it more likely that the request will not be turned down; in a religious community the word "profit" carries, presumably, less power.

Devil Words, on the other hand, frequently provoke a much stronger reaction in the listener (and there exist more of them) than God Words. While a God Word may *give* power to a person, idea, or event, Devil Words are said to *sap* the power away. Marketers have learned that Devil Words are repulsive or scary, so people turn away from products or behaviors connected with them. No one wants to be associated with those words. As a result, they become useful for attaching to the things that you want jurors to avoid, reject, or negatively judge.

Practice Tip: In civil and criminal trials, there are frequently groups or individuals that will react strongly to certain words:

- Find out what words trigger strong positive or negative associations for central characters in your case. (Jurors are always among the central characters.)
- Which God/Devil words can be used to trigger stronger reactions from jurors? Do some jurors have professional, religious, or life backgrounds that will make those words ring loudly?
- Are there God/Devil words that can be used, appropriately, to cross-examine or direct examine a witness? Influence a witness to adopt a claim that would otherwise be easily rejected?

Cross examination 1:

Attorney: Officer, your choice wasn't very *American*, was it?

Officer: What do you mean?

Attorney: In America, you don't get *special treatment* just because you have more money, now do you?

Officer: There was no special treatment! [Rejecting the Devil Words.]

Attorney: [Proceeds to list all the special treatment that was, in fact, given.]

SYMBOLIC THINKING

> **Cross examination 2:**
>
> **Attorney:** Doctor, what you told her was a flat out *lie*, wasn't it?
>
> **Doctor:** Well, no.
>
> **Attorney:** You don't want to say it was a lie, but it sure was not the *truth*, now was it?
>
> **Doctor:** It was a difficult situation, professionally.
>
> **Attorney:** "Do I have *cancer*?" Now which part of that question was confusing for you, doctor?
>
> **Doctor:** Her husband didn't want her to know.
>
> **Attorney:** The truth was that you had a solid diagnosis of cancer and your patient asked you about that, true?
>
> **Doctor:** Yes.
>
> **Attorney:** In *America*, a person has a right to the truth from their doctor, when they ask, now don't they!
>
> **Cross examination 3:**
>
> **Attorney:** You knew that picture was really *sacred* to your wife, didn't you?
>
> **Witness:** What do you mean?
>
> **Attorney:** It meant so much to her, because her mother had died. You knew that, true?
>
> **Witness:** Well, yes.
>
> **Attorney:** When you sell something that's *sacred* to someone else, that's just a little bit *evil*, wouldn't you say?

The most powerful practice tip available for these words is to collect them, create a notebook for them, and get people everywhere to give you more. Develop a hunger for these words; soon you will hear them in conversations, in films, on television, in hallways, on signs, in advertisements. Add them to your collection. To get you started, below is a general list, without any topical grouping, of powerful God/Devil words that would affect *most* people the same way:

JURY THINKING

Devil Words	God Words
nauseating	peace
pain	baby
scar	paradise
bankrupt	angel
malignant	church
disease	courage
poison	motherhood
waste	sacred
contaminated	holy
savage	prayer
sin/sinner	blessing
taboo	bonus
incest	gift
nightmare	treasure
criminal	hope
weed	faith
ghost	gold
haunted	music
kill/killer	Christmas
murder	springtime
death, dying	rainbow
rape	prize
catastrophe	smile

SYMBOLIC THINKING

Devil Words	God Words
blood	sunlight
fired	sacrifice
debt	cure
corrupt	helper
disfigure	compliment
death	kindness
coffin	rocking chair
monster	cottage
blind	crayons
crippled	caress
grave, graveyard	team
fool	fairness
funeral	beauty
doom	victory
tragedy	warmth
disaster	healer, healing
cancer	farmer
attack	carpenter
cholesterol	wisdom
dirty	innocence
curse/cursed	garden/gardener
terrorism/terrorist	soul
hunger	rescue

JURY THINKING

Devil Words	God Words
starvation	gratitude
thirst	thankfulness
neglect	dessert
germs	celebration
stress	harmony
tumor	patriotism
grief	pioneer
blackmail	champion
drunk	protector/protection
thief	mentor
criminal	miracle
manipulation	oasis
slavery	halo
bills	velvet
fist	hug
conflict	skill
forbidden	pride
rejection	guide
regret	trailblazer
tears	innovator
warning	morals
poverty	ethics
threat	comeback

SYMBOLIC THINKING

Devil Words	God Words
drown/drowning	remorseful
spoiled	redemption
humiliation	festival
ridicule	thrive
quit, quitter	salvation
swamp	underdog
earthquake	
tornado	
wildfire	
surgery	
hoax	
virus	
infection	
traitor	
spy	
torture	
deadline	
taxes	
suicide	
predator	
storm	
phobia	
fat	

JURY THINKING

Devil Words	God Words
scam	
garbage	
heart-attack	

The power of those words becomes immediately apparent, even when they are only read, not spoken. The key *tool*, however, in using them is not apparent:

TOOL = METAPHOR

You do not use "predator" to describe a hunter, but to describe a fellow employee whose behavior must be repulsive to a juror for you to prevail. You do not use "terrorism" to describe a battlefield maneuver, but to describe the behavior of a family member. As metaphors, God and Devil words give power in ways unexpected to the juror.

> **Practice Tip**: Use God or Devil words as:
> 1. adjectives (for a person, place, behavior, rule, outcome, expectation, plan)
> 2. comparisons (to differential people, ideas, outcomes, hopes, motives)
> 3. unlikely pairings

Rich sources of Devil Words come from our childhood, because they have affected us for a long, long time:

SYMBOLIC THINKING

Devil Words
copycat
tattletale
brat
quitter
cheating/cheater
bully
stingy

These are effective words to use for describing *adult* behaviors, simultaneously *infantilizing* someone and *demonizing* them. Childhood Devil Words have persuasive clout. Powerful in opening or closing, but strongest in cross-examination.

Practice Tip: Cross-examination using Childhood Devil Words.

Attorney: From what you say, officer, you were a *quitter* that night, weren't you?

Officer: [automatic rejection] No!

Attorney: Well, let's take a look at the choice you made. You had the choice to stay in the neighborhood, even though it was late, and knock on doors to see if anyone heard anything, no matter how long it took?

Another rich source for these persuasive words comes from the animal kingdom. We are using the Animal God/Devil Words, however, metaphorically. The list below also demonstrates effectively that while there are lovely canonized life forms, it's the demonized ones that have more power to get a reaction:

JURY THINKING

Devil Words	God Words
rat	puppy
snake	kitten
vulture	hummingbird
pig	lamb
dragon	unicorn
cockroach	butterfly
bugs	ladybugs
leech	cub
worm	swan
slug	dove
shark	dolphin

Interestingly, only a few God/Devil Words have direct *opposites*. That is, just because you have a clear Devil Word, it does not follow (rarely, in fact) that the opposite of that word is a God Word. Here's a few that DO have opposites:

Devil Words	God Words
betrayal	loyalty
coward, villain	hero
lie, deception	truth
loser	winner
homeless	home
greed	generosity
prison	freedom
rotten	fresh

SYMBOLIC THINKING

Devil Words	God Words
jail/jailer	savior
danger	safety
failure	success
criticism	praise
rudeness	courtesy
enemy	friend
victim	survivor
gang, clique	team
cruelty	kindness
despair, depression	hope
infidelity, adultery	loyalty
hell	heaven
forgotten	remembered
famine	feast
destroy	repair

On the other hand, here are Devil Words that demonstrate that their literal opposite is not, in fact, a powerful God Word:

Not So Much	
evil	[goodness]
disease, illness	[health]
divorce	[marriage]
mother	[father, sister, brother]
insanity	[sanity]

JURY THINKING

When a word is repulsive to *some* people under *some* circumstances, but not always, it is not a Devil Word. When a word is sacred to some people under some circumstances, but not always, it is not a God Word. This is, instead, an **it-all-depends word**, which means the word cannot be counted on. "Marriage," for example, does not evoke warm fuzzy feelings from all jurors; a "secret" can be delicious or deadly; "pregnancy" can be a much-sought-after miracle or a horrifying and complex development. **Practical tip:** Check out words with many people; your own view is likely slanted.

Words that Depend on Context for Emotion [Not necessarily bad, not necessarily good.]
silence
books
secret
Professions: priest, attorney, doctor, teacher, police
marriage
pregnant
army, soldier
science
religion
art
hospital
king
expert
weapon
medicine
food
smart

SYMBOLIC THINKING

Words that Depend on Context for Emotion **[Not necessarily bad, not necessarily good.]**
surprise
change
routine
rules
passion
work, play
candy
touch
news
law
justice
choice
rich, poor
laughter
solitude
childhood
contest, competition
tradition
technology

Since both God and Devil Words are most effective when they are used as metaphor, this is an excellent point at which to realize the ways in which a juror's thinking is uniquely affected by metaphor.

§ 4-2. Metaphor and Thought

> "Logic is a very elegant tool," he [Gregory Bateson] said, "and we've got a lot of mileage out of it for two thousand years or so. The trouble is, you know, when you apply it to crabs and porpoises and butterflies and habit formation . . . logic won't quite do, because that whole fabric of living things is not put together by logic. You see, when you get circular trains of causation (as you always do in the living world), the use of logic will make you walk into paradoxes."
>
> I got very excited and said with a provocative smile: "Heraclitus knew that! And so did Lao Tzu."
>
> "Yes, indeed; and so do the trees over there. Logic won't do for them."
>
> "So what do they use instead?"
>
> "Metaphor."
>
> "Metaphor?"
>
> "Yes, metaphor. That's how the whole fabric of mental interconnections holds together. Metaphor is right at the bottom of being alive."
>
> Capra, Uncommon Wisdom[40]

Over the past two decades, both cognitive and neuro-scientists have reached general agreement that the human brain's **conceptual system** contains thousands of metaphors—that are essential aids to help people understand concrete reality. Some scholars, in fact, now argue that without metaphoric thinking, humans could not engage in abstract thought at all—particularly thinking about causation, purpose, love, morality, or even thinking-about-thinking.[41] Metaphor is credited with the capacity to structure, transform, and create new knowledge, as well as evoke emotions and influence evaluations.

At a basic level, metaphors are **word comparisons**, of the form "A is B" (television is poison, the Rocky Mountains are heaven, love is magic). The fundamental feature of metaphor is the **passing of meaning** from B to A. The specific *persuasive effects* of metaphor were recently analyzed by Pradeep Sopory and James Price Dillard, who reviewed 41 published data-based studies from the social sciences.[42] They found that the use of metaphors does enhance persuasion, with the specific effects rising when a single metaphor was **novel** (but had a familiar target) and was used **early in the message**. In fact, metaphors were found to have a measurably greater impact on **attitude change** than **literal language**.

How does metaphor achieve its persuasive effects on an audience or listener? While a variety of theories have been offered, results across multiple studies supported the view that a metaphor helps the listener organize and make sense of the message, with **metaphor-as-theme** (at the outset of a persuasive pitch) most superior. Of particular usefulness to trial attorneys was the surprising finding that *metaphor is most persuasive in the audio (oral) form*, compared to written. This makes metaphor a rich tool for voir dire, opening statements, closing arguments, and, unexpectedly, cross-examinations.

There remains some disagreement about the degree to which people are aware of their brain's continual *metaphoric reasoning processes*. The general consensus emerging is that **conscious awareness of metaphoric thought**, when it occurs, is probably limited. Jurors may not be aware that they are reasoning, judging, or making sense of trial evidence by drawing upon their personal scrapbooks of metaphoric concepts—but it seems clear that when courtroom advocates Talk Metaphor, jurors listen more effectively. Metaphors have much-needed Velcro® power.

§ 4-2(a).   Metaphoric Thinking

It is important to look more carefully at how jurors will understand metaphorical expressions. Metaphor is so fundamental to human thought that research has found that even when adults are instructed to find "literal" meanings in words, people continue to find and rely upon metaphorical meanings.[43] It is, as a result, erroneous to assume that metaphoric thinking is a fallback strategy in a juror's brain, rather than an integral part of normal comprehension processes.

While metaphors are central to human thought, metaphoric thinking is never formally taught to us. People seem to think of metaphors as a natural human skill resulting in commonsense reasoning. Some scholars now point out an appealing intuition: that a faculty for analogical or metaphoric thinking is an innate part of human cognition.[44] Unfortunately, there is great variation both across and within cultures about the ways in which people use metaphor to categorize, reason, and make sense of their worlds. Attorneys who are multilingual, as far as metaphoric concepts are concerned, can more effectively create opening statements and closing arguments that appeal to diverse jurors. Steven Pinker has labeled mental concepts embedded in symbol and metaphor "mentalese," arguing that the language of thought has been overlooked by those attempting to understand how the mind works.[45]

So, what is a metaphor? A **metaphor** compares two seemingly unrelated things. Thus, a metaphor compares two things that are *literally quite unlike*, without using a comparison word. **One object is described as *being* a second object**:

> He had a heart of stone.
>
> The plan was a circus of errors.
>
> His training was a joke.

In this way, the first object is both economically and vividly described, drawing upon implicit and explicit attributes from the second object. The word "metaphor" derives from a Greek word that meant *transfer* or *transport* ("*meta*" which implies "change" and "*pherein*" which suggests "to bear or carry").

Metaphor differs from **simile**, for example, in that the explicit use of the words "like" or "as" are not used in a metaphor.[46] Metaphor relies on the verb "to be" and its persuasive power is derived from the claim that one thing *is* the other. Metaphor, as a result, is more forceful and more suggestive.

Practical Examples of Metaphor for Trial Lawyers:

He had the heart of a lion.

When he was criticized, he received it lightly, a fleeting shadow on a cloudy day.

The nurse was drowning in a sea of conflicting orders, the waves growing higher.

The silence was a blood-curdling scream of anguish.

The last broken promise cracked her soul.

His style of investigation was always crooked, but he never noticed.

She bent the truth so carefully, it almost went unnoticed.

They were steering the organization in different direction, frantically rowing in circles.

He raced through the consent advisement, trying only for a Personal Best time.

His values were limp and slippery; no one could ever get a grip on them.

When taken to an extreme, however, metaphoric talk may be called **hyperbole** (exaggeration) or **catachresis** (nonsense).

SYMBOLIC THINKING

> **Rhetorical caveats of courtroom metaphors**:
>
> On a practical level, trial advocates should pay attention to those two possibilities (hyperbole or catachresis) for two useful reasons: (a) a juror will reject any metaphor that is perceived to be an unreasonable exaggeration, and (b) when an adversary has engaged in metaphor, an appropriate reply might be to point out to the jury why the offered metaphor should be rejected as either an inappropriate exaggeration or an incomprehensible clump of diversionary images.

§ 4-2(b). Speaking in Metaphor

A spoken metaphor functions to make an event or issue being described more vivid in the mind of the listener/juror (and, as a result, more *believable*):

> The mechanism by which spirituality becomes passionate is metaphor. An ineffable God requires metaphor not only to be imagined but to be approached, exhorted, evaded, confronted, struggled with, and loved. Through metaphor, the vividness, intensity, and meaningfulness of ordinary experience becomes the basis of a passionate spirituality. An effable God becomes vital through metaphor: The Supreme Being. The Prime Mover. The Creator. The Almighty. The Father. The King of Kings. Shepherd. Potter. Lawgiver. Judge. Mother. Lover. Breath.[47]

Lakoff and Johnson[48] point out that metaphoric language is a vehicle by which people are moved within a realm of passionate spirituality. Since many of the ultimate requests trial attorneys make of jurors will be affected by the passion and spiritual values triggered in individual jurors, the ability to *speak in metaphor* is an essential advocacy skill: describing a plaintiff's pain or loss, requesting punitive damages, arguing against the death penalty as a sentence, urging the jury to think of the greater issues embedded in their verdict, suggesting that a behavior must be condemned, exposing a complex lie, requesting an unpopular choice, to name a few. The mechanism of metaphor is bodily, that is, it produces a type of **somatic persuasion** [concept introduced in § 5-4, PRACTICAL JURY DYNAMICS]. Any metaphor is effective because it triggers a *neural mechanism* in a listener's brain and this neural activity facilitates a listener's (juror's) ability to mentally perceive, to move, to feel, or to envision—not only by producing traditional sequential/logical thought, but also by producing spiritual, value-laden thinking. Effective metaphors stimulate more frequent **Velcro® Effect** (§ 5-5, PRACTICAL JURY DYNAMICS) than plain language can produce.

§ 4-2(c).   Types of Metaphoric Talk

John Casnig is a multidisciplinary metaphoric thinker who generously shares his ideas on the Internet (www.knowgramming.com; permission for us to adapt his work here). Casnig invites us to pay attention to **sensory metaphors**, in particular, which bolsters my previous practical courtroom tips that a juror's personal **sensory memory** is powerful (§ 3-2, PRACTICAL JURY DYNAMICS) and, further, that **sensual persuasion** by lawyers is superior to *event* persuasion (§ 5-4, PRACTICAL JURY DYNAMICS).

Among the most common metaphors (therefore jurors will be familiar with them) are those that refer to our senses of touch, taste, sight, hearing, and smell. Many of our everyday spoken phrases are metaphor. Casnig points out that sensory metaphoric opportunities do not stop with human sensory experience, since *machines* have sensory devices as well (i.e., many parts are actually named according to metaphors reflective of the human sensory experience, such as "electric eye" or " feelers").

EXAMPLES OF SENSORY METAPHORS:

TEMPERATURE/TOUCH

Hunka' hunka' **burnin'** love.

An old **flame**.

There's a **fire** in my heart and you fan it, Janet.

Boiling mad.

A **feverish** pace.

I'm so **hot** for her and she's so cold.

Heated debate.

A **warm** reception.

A **tepid** speech.

Chill out!!

Cool!

An **icy** stare.

Frozen with fear.

The news **inflamed** her temper.

They were **kindling** a new romance.

A **hot** piece of gossip.

COLOR/LIGHT

Feeling **blue**.

Green with envy.

You **light** up my life.

The **blackest** thoughts.

Only shades of **grey**.

A **colorful** remark.

Dark secrets.

A **rainbow** of choices.

An infinite **spectrum** of possibilities.

A **bright** idea.

A **dim** view.

He **faded** off to sleep.

I fail to **see** your logic.

Memory **clouded** by time.

His morals were **hazy**.

The **light** of reason.

A **shining** example of heroism.

A **yellow** coward.

A **red** letter day.

A **green** thumb in the garden.

A **golden** opportunity missed.

TASTE

She was **sweet** but clueless.

He opened the gift with **bitterness.**

Bittersweet memories danced in her head.

Ending on a **sour** note.

He displayed unfortunate **taste** in romances.

His words had sharp **bite** to them.

You've given me something to **chew** on.

He found her behavior **unpalatable**.

His ideas were remarkably **bland**.

He was the **salt** of the earth.

TEXTURE

That has been **hard** to do.

He **felt** her sadness.

Her **soft** voice was music to his ears.

The author's **gritty** style.

His **silken** lies went unheard.

Things are going **smoothly**.

He had a **coarse** manner of speech.

Her voice is beginning to **grate** on me.

That's a **rough** break; too bad.

Her words were **velvet** to his ears.

His glare was **sharp** and cutting.

His style was **slimy**.

His old hands were **leather**.

SYMBOLIC THINKING

> ### SMELL
>
> Love **stinks**.
>
> The **sweet smell** of success.
>
> The **stench** of failure.
>
> The man **reeked** of infidelity.
>
> The decision was **fetid** and stale.
>
> The deal didn't **smell** right.
>
> His words were **perfume**.
>
> Suddenly, he **smelled** unfamiliar defeat.
>
> The investigator **sniffed** out the details.
>
> ### SOUND
>
> The room **listened**.
>
> No one was leading the **orchestra** in that army.
>
> It went all wrong, somehow **off key**.
>
> He **heard** a different drummer.
>
> Her words **rang** true.
>
> The letter was **music** to his ears.
>
> The **high note** of the evening.
>
> She **thundered** into the room.
>
> Her touch was **whisper** soft.
>
> Their conversation became **jazz**.
>
> Something in the conversation was clearly **flat**.
>
> Their relationship had been a long **waltz**.

Metaphors are also powerful, however, because they can indirectly communicate much more than information and evaluation. Metaphors can trigger **emotions**, which is critical in many trials in order for either a plaintiff or defendant to prevail. Organizations have long attempted to use the metaphor "family" rather than work group to increase commitment of workers, for example. Metaphors can provide amusement, as well—and humorous metaphors are best remembered.[49]

§ 4-2(d). Complex Metaphoric Phrases

Metaphors are so powerful that when they are *phrased* they can grab you like a great book title. Metaphoric phrasing involves a complex system of relationships. Casnig calls them Complex Metaphorical Systems.

> **Practice Tip: Theme a client's case with metaphor.** While many of us recognize the value of coming up with a colorful book title for our cases, we neglect to use the powerful metaphors available to make these titles more vivid, more retrievable, and more familiar to jurors. Consider these potential "book titles" that focus a juror's attention, create themes, and suggest appropriate judgment:
>
> CARDIOVASCULAR SURGERY ON A POOL TABLE
>
> THE INTERNAL COMBUSTION RESTAURANT
>
> PLAYING WORMHOLE CHESS
>
> THE GENETICS OF ALPHABET SOUP
>
> A CIRCUS OF CLOWNS DESIGNING A PROCEDURE
>
> A FATAL SPELL OF INATTENTION
>
> CAUGHT IN AN UNFAMILIAR FOREST
>
> A CASE OF TOXIC FRIENDS AND TOO-FRIENDLY TOXINS
>
> A COMEDY OF ERRORS IN A DRAMA OF RISKS
>
> HER SENDER WAS BROKEN AND HIS RECEIVER WAS BENT
>
> HE OFFERED A TWILIGHT ZONE OF EXCUSES
>
> SHE GOT THE GOLD MINE, HE GOT THE SHAFT

Each of these "themes" for a witness, an event, a defense at trial uses a metaphoric phrase as a **stepping stone** to help a juror understand some other concept or issue. **Mental linking** occurs, joining an event (or lack of an event) to its meaning or interpretation. Juror thinking is facilitated.

SYMBOLIC THINKING

Metaphors remain under-utilized instruments of communication to jurors in courtroom advocacy.

> ***Practice Tip.*** Metaphoric talk among jurors in the juryroom during group argument can be powerful:
>
> THE ATTORNEY WHO PLANTS AND WATERS METAPHORS DURING TRIAL HAS THE GREATEST CHANCE OF HARVESTING SOME OF THEM DURING JURY DELIBERATIONS.

It follows that it is far more important that the message be conveyed to jurors, than it is for all content metaphors to be continuous or connected. **Patchwork metaphors** (just like *Crazy Quilts*, p. 37, PRACTICAL JURY DYNAMICS), using a variety of sensual images, work well for some jurors. You may need to jump freely from metaphor to metaphor.[7] When swimming in metaphoric seas, it is worth paying attention to risks, as well as rich goals.

Caveat: An important point to remember is that communicating a metaphor depends upon a **shared background knowledge**. If a juror (even one juror) is unfamiliar with the suggested "source" of comparison, metaphoric thinking will not happen.

One of the key principles of persuading other people relies on one simple premise: *when you change how someone thinks about a thing, you change how that person will see it.* Robert Stetson Shaw said it well:[50]

> YOU WON'T SEE SOMETHING
> UNTIL YOU HAVE THE RIGHT METAPHOR TO LET YOU PERCEIVE IT.

---

[7]. When in doubt about the effectiveness of a possible Patchwork Metaphor, check with a nine-year-old. They know everything.

Types of Metaphor		
Type	**Definition**	**Example**
Extended	Sets up a principal subject with several subsidiary subjects or comparisons.	Dinners in their family were a battlefield, where attacks were unexpected, shrapnel flew through the air, and words were deadly bullets.
Mixed	Leaps between different comparisons.	Practicing medicine for him was sometimes a treasure of unexpected richness, but mistakes lurked in the shadows, and criticism was toxic.
Dead	The original image associated with the word has been lost, so the metaphoric power is not present for the listener. The word is familiar, the original comparison object is lost.	"Consideration" was a metaphor originally meaning "take the stars into account." "Gorge" meant throat. "Mantel" meant "cloak to catch smoke."
Active	Contrasts with "dead" metaphors because the comparison is not typically used in daily language.	Her friendship is poison. The effort was pale. The relationship was toxic.
Anti-metaphor	An ineffective metaphor because there is no obvious resemblance between the two images.	The surgery was a moon. The contract read like a Girl Scout. *[Listener reaction: Huh?]*
Loose	Effectiveness lies in its ability to catch the mind with several points of similarity to the object of comparison.	Her injury was a cross to bear every hour of the day. *[Suggesting heaviness, pain, public martyrdom.]*
Implicit	A subtle type of metaphor that avoids saying "A is B" and instead says, "A has the following strange qualities," which implies those qualities belong to B.	Deceit slithered quietly into the courtroom and coiled itself into the witness chair. *[Nowhere does it actually say "Deceit is a snake" but that is implied, as well as "The witness is a snake."]*

SYMBOLIC THINKING

\	Types of Metaphor	
Type	**Definition**	**Example**
SUBMERGED METAPHOR	In this type of metaphor, the comparison object is implied.	His eyes flew through the inspection. *[The audience must supply the image of an airplane or bird.]*
TIGHT METAPHOR	The metaphor only draws upon one point of resemblance between the two objects.	"Hot head." [Temperature is the comparison object in the metaphor, but nothing about temperature except "hot" is referenced, so the listener can only connect the person referred to by one attribute of temperature.
ROOT METAPHOR	This metaphor relies upon personal value systems (which shape a person's understanding or judgments), rather than any explicit language device. Its power lies in triggering multiple comparisons that are then filtered through personal value systems.	Examples of root metaphors: religion, liberal, conservative. "He's a liberal doctor." *[The attributes conveyed by "liberal" depend on the listener's political root metaphor; is it a good or bad thing to be considered liberal?]*

The metaphor is perhaps one of man's most fruitful potentialities. Its efficacy verges on magic and it seems a tool for creation, which God forgot inside one of his creatures, when he made him.

Jose Ortega y Gasset[51]

Chapter 5

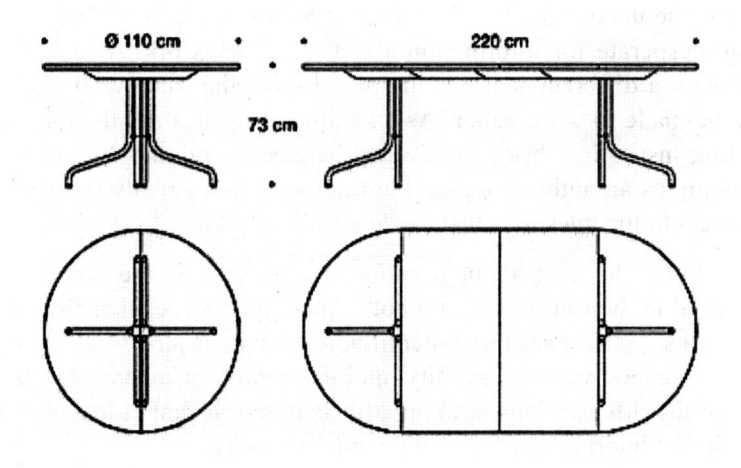

STRUCTURES THAT INFLUENCE THINKING

Jurors may, or may not, be capable of *approaching* impartiality in any particular trial, but we know jurors are profoundly influenced by some factors that are, indeed, outside either the realm of either evidence or the legal instructions. The **geography** of both the courtroom and juryroom are two of them. Architecture, design, positions, shape, and relationship of objects to other objects all influence how a juror will think and communicate with other jurors. Furniture is worth paying attention to for other than aesthetic motivations. [See § 5-2(b), below, *Reform Structures Missing from the ABA Principles*].

First, however, we will examine recent studies that illuminate some of the *thinking structures* that influence juror decision making during trial.

§ 5-1. Jury Studies: Updates

While a complete review of all jury studies published in the last two years is beyond the scope of this update, a number of studies merit attention. Below are issues upon which there is recent research worth giving attention to, depending upon the trial issues you face:

§ 5-1(a). Jury Instructions

Professor John Conley at the University of North Carolina School of Law is both a lawyer and an anthropologist who offers wonderful insights into jury thinking and legal instructions:

> I view the understanding of juries as a holy grail. When thinking tactically, I am desperate for information about how they work. As a law teacher, I focus on a different sense of that word—whether they work and how they can be made to work better. As an anthropologist, I see the jury as a legitimating institution, bridging the gap between legal and lay cultures. When thinking as an anthropologist, I am not sure that I really want to know the answers to the questions that my legal self is asking.[52]

- Jurors' thinking about insanity is influence by the "prototypes" they hold in their heads that are not related to either legal or psychiatric concepts.[53] There are three identifiable groups of jurors that think in terms of: severe mental disability, moral insanity, or mental state at the time of the offense. This thinking affects case-relevant attitudes and the way jurors interpret evidence and render verdicts.

- Most studies find that jurors do not understand the law as it is presented to them in court. Decades of social science research on the effects of the jury instruction process were examined[54] and provide specific findings from both civil and criminal trials, all of which support eliminating pattern instructions.

§ 5-1(b). Own Race Bias

- What better evidence can there be to influence a juror's trial thinking than "I saw him, that's the man!" pointing at the defendant in a courtroom? Thirty years of social science research has supported an own-race bias in witness memory for faces. What we have not done is bring that home to jurors during jury selection, in bite-sized digested pieces. What we have not done is engage jurors in a discussion of those results and explore with them their own thinking about own-race bias and memory for faces. An excellent resource is the Meissner and Brigham work:[55] all you need to know as of 2001. This is a great resource, reader-friendly, with highly relevant examples from the courtroom.

STRUCTURES THAT INFLUENCE THINKING

§ 5-1(c). Personal Injury Damage Awards

- When a juror is first offered an anchor point, a new fact will be considered good or bad, high or low, by comparing it to that fact (§ 2-2, Brain Facts/Mind Facts, PRACTICAL JURY DYNAMICS). One study found that award size and variability increased as the plaintiff's request increased—but decreased with more extreme requests.[56] Conversely, award size decreased when the defense rebuttal decreased, yet increased with "extreme" rebuttals. When award recommendations were offered to the jury, the upper and lower boundaries of awards the jurors found acceptable changed (though an award recommendation did not affect perception of injury severity). It appears award recommendations do produce a change in juror thinking, beyond the facts or law of the case.

§ 5-1(d). Expectation Effects

- There is more evidence that jurors cannot disregard what is in plain view for them to experience. Even when admonished to disregard a trial judge's verbal/nonverbal behavior and form their own opinions, jurors returned verdicts consistent with the judges' preferences. There were magnified effects when the jurors were given the instruction in advanced of the anticipated testimony (a primacy effect).[57]

§ 5-1(e). Lay Representations of Legal Concepts

- The assumption that jurors have no prior knowledge of the law or will set such knowledge aside may not be justified. Research found that jurors had built naïve representations of crime categories that included legally incorrect information, that these influenced their verdict choices, and that the jurors' reliance on their own prototype information for verdict selection was *resistant to change by instruction*.[58] Jurors had prior knowledge of the law and did not set it aside after hearing the judge's instructions, suggesting that judicial instructions must do more than create legal concepts were none exist (elements)—to be effective, instructions must address and reverse the existing thinking jurors have about legal concepts.

§ 5-1(f). Effect of Judicial Warnings During Trial

- The younger the child, the more likely that a jury will believe that child, under some conditions. A judicial warning about the age of a witness had no impact on guilty verdicts when a 7-year-old was a witness, but seemed to reduce the guilty verdicts when the child witness was 10 years old or 23 (young adult).[59] Interestingly, the jurors did associate the younger child with lower cognitive competence and higher suggestibility, but also with higher accuracy of recall. It appears that a juror's thinking has several levels concerning child witnesses and detailed inquiry during voir dire is warranted.

§ 5-1(g). Reading Minds of Others (Mental States)

- It is difficult for a juror to read the mind of a stranger, generally a trial witness, plaintiff, or defendant, yet trials ask them to make judgments about what others want, think, feel, intend. Here a useful model is described (the Mind Reader's Tool Kit) based upon the results of three supporting studies: when people perceived themselves as similar to a target, they engaged in higher levels of projection and lower levels of stereotyping in mental state inferences than when they perceived themselves as dissimilar. Jurors, at appears, may use "perceived similarity" to a witness or party to help them organize their judgments.[60]

§ 5-1(h). How Jurors Use/Misuse Character Evidence

- The introduction of evidence of positive defendant character did not, surprisingly, affect guilt judgments. Cross-examination of a defendant's character witnesses caused a backlash in which juror judgments were harsher than when no character evidence was offered.[61]

§ 5-1(i). Notetaking

- Six-person juries that did not take notes during trial awarded multiple plaintiffs the highest compensation and gave the highest punitive damages. Multiple plaintiffs increased the unpredictability of jury punitive awards. Twelve-person juries deliberated longer, recalled more probative information and relied less on improper evidence.[62]

STRUCTURES THAT INFLUENCE THINKING

§ 5-1(j). Hearing and Believing Hearsay Evidence.

The rules of evidence (including hearsay testimony) are not grounded in scientific research about how jurors think, but, instead, evolved over a period of three centuries from American and British legal traditions. It is not surprising, as a result, that we know little about how hearsay objections by attorneys (and the subsequent rulings of judges) impact the thinking of trial jurors. The Federal Rules of Evidence, in fact, recognize twenty-nine specific situations that permit the introduction of hearsay testimony.[63]

> Practically speaking, trial attorneys should consider whether *significant hearsay evidence* is likely to be admitted at trial, then, whether such evidence *harms or helps* the client.

Either way, the **nature of hearsay testimony** ought to be discussed with the jurors during voir dire (or, if that is not possible, during opening statement).[*] "Hearsay" is not commonly understood by lay people, nor do objections to proposed hearsay make obvious sense.

> When jurors must guess about what hearsay is in the courtroom moment, and, further, must individually speculate about *whether it is either reasonable or sneaky* for an attorney to object to it or to offer it, clients can be unnecessarily hurt.

WHAT EVERY JUROR SHOULD KNOW ABOUT HEARSAY EVIDENCE

- Our courts believe that **live testimony by a witness under oath** is more accurate than someone repeating what someone else supposedly said or saw.

- Jurors have a right to **eye-to-eye confrontation** with every witness.

- Jurors have a right to observe a **witness's demeanor** while testifying, since twitches, hesitancies, shifts, quiverings, glances, sneers, and tone of voice reveal deception or truth-telling, as well as confidence or uncertainty.

- Jurors have a right to see how the person who actually said something handles **adversarial cross-examination**, which can reveal malice or bias.

---

* A *discussion* is not the same as a *lecture*. A discussion shares thoughts. A discussion involves listening, as well as talking.

JURY THINKING

> • **Meaning is lost** when someone is only repeating what someone else supposedly said or saw.

It is practical and useful to find out whether jurors believe these concepts, dispute them, or can offer examples from their own lived experiences. It is particularly useful to jurors to **think about this rationale before any hearsay is admitted or denied**. Closing argument is too late. Even cross-examination or re-direct or re-cross may be, in fact, too late, since a juror's brain is already absorbing the impact and making assumptions. The hearsay testimony and the arguments about the testimony are already being filed in **retrievable folders** in a juror's brain.

An excellent review and critique of empirical studies that have been done about how people react to hearsay evidence was done in 1999 by Professor McGough,[64] who argues for revision of the legal doctrine of the hearsay rule and its exceptions.

§ 5-1(k). Juror Thinking About Witness Memory.

Trials always involve issues about the accuracy of one or more witnesses' memory. *Jury thinking* about any witness's memory requires an understanding of mental schemas (§ 7-3, event schemas; § 7-4, influence of juror's categories and schemas; § 3-2, expectations filling memory gaps, PRACTICAL JURY DYNAMICS). Once again, cross-examination that attacks a witness's memory is too late to un-persuade most jurors; they were already *blinking towards believing* the witness. Avoid having to un-blink the jurors when you plan to attack the memory of an opponent's witness.

It is important to talk about what might affect a witness's memory, but, perhaps more important, it is important to discuss and put on the juror's mental table the concept of **memory decay**.

> Jurors who do not believe that human memory decay is normal, unavoidable, and probable under certain circumstances present *a challenge for cause opportunity*.

> **WHAT EVERY JUROR NEEDS TO KNOW ABOUT WITNESS MEMORY**
> • A **schema-pattern** is a mental short-cut all people use to make quick comparisons to past information or experiences.
> • **All people** hold schemas in their minds for different events or people.

STRUCTURES THAT INFLUENCE THINKING

> - A witness's mental **schema-pattern affects their memory** about anything.
> - A witness's memory is affected by **how soon they are asked to recall** something.
> - A witness's memory is affected by **how many times they are asked to recall** something.
> - A witness's memory is affected by the **order of questions** they are asked.
> - A witness's memory is affected by **what other people say they remember**.
> - A witness's memory is affect by **approval** or disapproval.
> - Memory **decays after an event**.
> - Memory is **less accurate when the time before the first interview increases**.
> - Memory decay occurs more often for events that were **different than the schema-patterns** a person was expecting or had experienced before.
> - Just because a witness feels **certain** does not make the memory accurate.

A useful study investigating the specific influence of schemas, stimulus ambiguity, and interview question order on **eyewitness memory over time** was published in 2003 by Professors Michelle Tuckey and Neil Brewer,[65] which also provides a summary of prior studies to that date. It offers scientific support for the above truths.

Age stereotyping affects juror thinking. The age of an eyewitness may affect a juror's thinking about witness believability. *Are older eyewitnesses more or less believable according to the thinking of jurors?* In a recent study, young adults rated an 82-year-old female witness to be **less competent** but **more honest** than a 28-year-old female witness.[66] This is significant because the more competent a witness was perceived as being, the more influential was the *misinformation* that witness provided. Negative beliefs a juror may hold that associate incompetence with old age may compromise the believability of an older eyewitness before they have a chance to testify.

> **Practice Tip: Elicit Beliefs about Age.**
>
> If you are offering an older witness: (a) get this study and read it, (b) draft an instruction for the court to give during trial disabusing jurors of the idea that age necessarily affects witness competency, (c) find out during jury selection (orally or on a questionnaire) who may hold such a belief, *even a little*, and (d) pursue challenges for cause based upon *negative beliefs that associate incompetence with old age.*

§ 5-1(l). Effects of Defendant Conduct on Jury Thinking About Damage Awards

Jurors in civil negligence trials are expected by law to determine compensatory damages by assessing the severity of a plaintiff's injuries, but not by considering the conduct of a defendant. In fact, however, jurors may think (and vote) differently.

Tort law requires that damages should be influenced only by the severity of the plaintiff's injuries, not the reprehensibility of defendant's conduct. In fact, however, when a plaintiff's injuries are severe, there may be a **jury demonization effect**. That is, while a juror is able to think separately about the plaintiff's injury and defendant's conduct when the injury to the plaintiff was mild, *under circumstances when a plaintiff's injury was severe and a defendant's conduct was "very careless" jurors inappropriate merge information about conduct into the thinking about damage awards*. One study recently supported this phenomenon.

Jurors in simulated civil negligence cases were found to assess damages under strong influence by the severity of a plaintiff's injuries, as well as the conduct of a defendant.[67] Jurors indeed appear to be unable to **un-think** the evidence heard at trial about a defendant's conduct. One explanation may be that some jurors think using the **hindsight bias**. According to the hindsight bias, people find it difficult to un-think information that they already have.

> *Jurors influenced by the hindsight bias are unable to disregard information about the defendant's conduct during damage assessment and they cannot reproduce the thinking they would have made if they did not have that information!*

Significantly for all trials, both civil and criminal, this study found NO support for the notion that group deliberations would "correct" the improper thinking of individual jurors. Individual pre-deliberation thinking that was contrary to the jury instructions was still reflected in individual post-deliberation thinking.

If civil jurors will augment a damage award according to the reprehensibility of a defendant's conduct, it can be expected that jurors in a criminal case may lower the burden of proof in cases where the defendant's conduct was perceived as particularly atrocious (even though the elements of the crime and the intent remain the same for criminal behavior that was less loathsome).

Practice Tip: Instruct, re-instruct, snitch.

It appears that jurors must be instructed early, often, and in everyday language.

- Options: Pre-voir dire instructions by the court with real world examples, allowing attorneys to talk to jurors about that aspect of the law.
- Voir dire on the hindsight bias.
- Re-instruction before any witness testifies about damages.
- Re-instruction at the close of the case.
- Re-instruction by during closing argument, with concrete examples of what thinking must be disregarded, however tempting.
- Let the jurors know what to do if the law is, in fact, disregarded (the snitch instruction). Send a note out immediately that the subject came up during deliberations.
- Re-instruct if the note comes out.
- Move for mistrial if the jury note appears to adversely affect your client and the content of the note indicates that one or more jurors have, in fact, disregarded the law.

---

§ 5-2. Jury Reform

§ 5-2(a). ABA 2005 Principles for Juries and Jury Trial

In the spring of 2005, the House of Delegates and the Board of Governors of the American Bar Association approved the "Principles for Juries and Jury Trials" proposed in a cooperative national project by the American Jury Project. *[The full text of these principles appears in the appendix.]* The preamble to the

Principles makes it clear that jury thinking and innovative reforms that emerge from thinking about jurors are encouraged:

> The American jury is *a living institution* that has played a crucial part in our democracy for more than two hundred years. The American Bar Association recognizes the legal community's *ongoing need to refine and improve jury practice* so that the right to jury trial is preserved and *juror participation enhanced*. What follows is a set of 19 principles that define our fundamental aspirations for the management of the jury system. Each principle is designed to express the best of current-day jury practice in light of existing legal and practical constraints. It is anticipated that over the course of the next decade jury practice will improve so that the *principles set forth will have to be updated* in a manner that will draw them ever closer to the principles to which we aspire. [Emphasis added.]

The ABA's **preamble** provides several excellent supporting principles for an attorney's request for special jury conditions, and these should be included in any motions (oral or written). Many of the various ABA standards have been cited by the United States Supreme Court as appropriate authorities.

While it is beyond the scope of this year's update to analyze each of the new Principles, a number of them fit into the reformist thinking and problematizing already introduced in both JURY THINKING and in PRACTICAL JURY DYNAMICS. These are summarized below. *The alerts offered to Principles should be read with the realization that the saliency of these issues will differ across cases; however, since some attorneys are representing people facing the death penalty and others are speaking for clients whose entire livelihood, health, or future is impacted by the verdict, it is important to acknowledge what a complete fair trial might look like, in light of these new principles.*

ABA Jury Principle	Jury Thinking
Principle 2(E): Courts should provide an adequate and suitable environment for jurors.	*Motions* that request specific jurors' health needs are met, in terms of breaks, chairs, opportunities to eat frequently, standing-stretching, access to medicines or medical devices, hearing or visual enhancement, length of breaks/lunch hours, total hours in court day, opportunities to communicate with dependent family members, and transportation needs, to name a few.

STRUCTURES THAT INFLUENCE THINKING

ABA Jury Principle	Jury Thinking
	Questionnaires that ask jurors what conditions they have that will make jury service burdensome in any way, then requesting a description of accommodations they need in all of these areas to make their jury service less burdensome. *Court instructions at the outset* informing the jurors that their lives may change and when they need new accommodations, schedules, or opportunities, they should immediately inform the court.
Principle 3(A): Juries in civil cases should be constituted of 12 members wherever possible and under no circumstances fewer than six members.	*Motions* detailing how it would be possible to have 12 members appears particularly advantageous to the party who does not have the burden of proof, since a jury of 12 may not agree as readily as a jury of 6 that a burden has been met. If the motion is denied, it is critical for future cases and appeal that the trial judge set forth on the record *all* the reasons Principle 3(A) was not possible for this trial.
Principle 3(B)(1): Juries in criminal cases should consist of twelve persons if a penalty of confinement for more than six months may be imposed upon conviction.	*Motions* in advance of trial for 12-person juries can be made in states that previously had fewer in criminal cases (for example 6 jurors in Florida or 8 in Arizona). *Motions* for 12-person juries can be made for juvenile cases, especially where the charge would be a crime if committed by an adult and "confinement" is the likely outcome. All *reasons* for a denial of such a motion must be requested, on the record. Further, ask the judge what additional evidence or law would be considered for a favorable ruling. A blanket denial appears inappropriate in light of Principle 3(B)(1). *Motions* challenging any state court rules or statutes concerning juries that detail fewer

ABA Jury Principle	Jury Thinking
	than 12 should be challenged as unconstitutional, offering in support the extensive testimony and rationale used by the ABA in endorsing this radical change.
Principle 4(A): In civil cases, ***jury decisions should be unanimous wherever possible.*** A less-than-unanimous decision should be accepted only after jurors have deliberated for a reasonable period of time and if concurred in by at least five-sixths of the jurors.	The wording of this principle suggests some within-committee controversy and lacks relevant specifics, so the creative burden is now on litigators to ask for what your client and the case needs. • In advance of trial, a request can be made to the trial judge to define guidelines for determining *"a reasonable period of time"* and what authorities or history would be relied upon for that finding. What will be the relevant variables considered? What training has the court had or authorities presented at recent judicial conferences on this point? Who had the burden of persuasion in arguing the matter to the court? • What will the jurors be told and when will they be told it? Jurors informed at the outset that their verdict must be unanimous have *different* deliberations than those who are told that less than unanimity might apply. Deliberations and the persuasion burden during decision-making will be impacted. • How many jurors is 5/6 of 8, for example?
Principle 5(A)(3): Responsibility for administering the jury system should be vested in a single administrator or clerk *acting under the supervision of a presiding judge of the court.*	Many courts have delegated the assembly and excusal of jury venires to jury commissioners (some of whom have, in turn, delegated to clerks). A delegation of responsibility without guidelines, dialogue, and specifics would be improper. Here, authority exists for supervision (presumably a direct form of communication on a regular basis).

STRUCTURES THAT INFLUENCE THINKING

ABA Jury Principle	Jury Thinking
	• Consider a hearing (challenging the venire), at which the jury commissioner is called as a witness to explain what supervision is given, by whom, what written guidelines are offered, and how the office responds to specific citizen requests. Some jury offices routinely excuse people over a certain age, with a certain number of children, or those who have to drive a certain distance, for example, and these are not made on the record. Consider also calling one or more members of the staff, sequestered, to see who they are excusing over the phone and with what guidelines. The Chief Judge of the court is also an appropriate witness on the issue of what was delegated, in what form, and what supervision and regular feedback occurs.
Principle 5(B): Courts should collect and analyze information regarding the performance of the jury system on a regular basis in order to endure . . . representativeness, inclusiveness, effectiveness, responsiveness to summonses, efficient use of jurors, and disability accommodations.	Is this happening? How often, with what data? Has anything changed since the new ABA Principles were adopted? Particularly alarming is the way a jury venire can be skewed when there is no regular immediate action for **failure to respond to a jury summons**.
Principle 10: Courts should use open, fair and flexible procedures to select a representative pool of prospective jurors.	While this is tedious for the jury commissioner's office, failure to respond to a summons can be due to moving, renters, nondrivers, multi-person living situations where mail is lost or not delivered, and students (parents do not forward the summons), to name a few. Interview the jury office clerks and collect data. What percentage of citizens did not respond to the summons in the last call? Last 3 months?

ABA Jury Principle	Jury Thinking
	Last 12 months? Are records kept of who those people are (names, addresses may suggest ethnicity or social economic levels)? Venires can be challenged on the basis that (a) there is no data kept, or (b) there is no effective follow up for failure to respond (allowing citizens to opt out).
Principle 6(A): Courts should provide orientation and preliminary information to persons called for jury service upon initial contact prior to service, upon fist appearance at the courthouse, and upon reporting to a courtroom for juror voir dire.	• Gather the specific information mailed to jurors with the summons, including any Web sites they are directed to. • Gather all information distributed by the jury office. • Gather all video, slides, films shown to orient jurors. • Gather all oral remarks and guidelines for those remarks made by anyone. • Some orientation material is appropriate for a civil case but not a criminal case, or the reverse. Read the material with your case in mind. • Some orientation material may improperly suggest how the jurors should deliberate, how they should select a foreperson, or how the deliberations and voting should proceed.
Principle 6(B)(2): Orientation programs should be presented in a uniform and efficient manner using a combination of written, oral, and audiovisual materials.	Consider objecting to oral remarks by anyone. They cannot possibly be presented in a uniform manner. How do they answer oral questions by citizens who show up? Do they record them?
Principle 10(A): Juror source pools should be assembled so as to assure representativeness and inclusiveness.	There has been no clear comparison base developed for determining representativeness.

STRUCTURES THAT INFLUENCE THINKING

ABA Jury Principle	Jury Thinking
Principle 10(A)(4): Should the court determine that improvement is needed in the representativeness or inclusiveness of the jury source list or the assembled jury pool, appropriate corrective action should be taken.	Some courts use census numbers, but these are frequently more than 10 years old. Gather the best comparison data you can, from multiple sources, to challenge the venire based on a failure to represent the population AT THE TIME OF TRIAL. Chambers of Commerce, schools, colleges, assessors, civil organizations, marketing groups all have data. If a mall is built, a restaurant opened, a new Wal-Mart appears, there is fresh data about the demographics of the projected customers. Do not rely upon old census demographics.
Principle 11(A): Before voir dire begins, the court and parties, through the use of appropriate questionnaires, should be provided with data pertinent to the eligibility of jurors and to matters ordinarily raised in voir dire … **Principle 11(A)(1):** In appropriate cases, the court should consider using a specialized questionnaire addressing particular issues that may arise. The court should permit the parties to submit a proposed juror questionnaire … **Principle 11(A)(3):** All completed questionnaires should be provided to the parties in sufficient time before the start of voir dire to enable the parties to adequately review them before the start of that examination.	Questionnaires are clearly endorsed, beyond simple demographics. Case specific issues are not only mandated, but adequate time for the parties to read them. However, for some judges this will be new. It benefits attorneys to raise this issue well-ahead of trial (first appearance is not too soon), to ask the court to talk about new thinking in light of the 2005 ABA Principles: *How can we work together to help this happen, judge?*

ABA Jury Principle	Jury Thinking
Principle 11(B)(2): Following initial questioning by the court, each party should have the opportunity, under the supervision of the court and subject to reasonable time limits, to question jurors directly, both individually and as a panel. **Principle 11(B)(3):** Voir dire should be sufficient to disclose grounds for challenges for cause *and to facilitate intelligent exercise of peremptory challenges.*	In some jurisdictions, this is a radical departure, but the language is strong, that is, "should." Both the books PRACTICAL JURY DYNAMICS and JURY THINKING set out detailed, issue-specific voir dire questions. File a motion well-before trial if this has not been happening: you need to know what the judge's thinking is and what you can offer to get what your client needs.
Principle 13(A)(1): Jurors should be allowed to take notes during trial ... and should receive appropriate cautionary instructions on note-taking and note use...	Since jurors stop observing the demeanor of witnesses when they take notes, miss portions of testimony when they take notes, and are not certified to take accurate notes, the taking of notes impairs a juror's trial task.
Principle 13(A)(2): Jurors should ordinarily be permitted to use their notes throughout the trial and during deliberations.	All four video-taped jury deliberations reported in PRACTICAL JURY DYNAMICS showed that even though each jury was instructed to only use their notes for their own memory—the rule was not followed. Jurors shared notes, read notes out loud, commented on valuing the notes of one another. *As a result, more instruction is needed.* An attorney or judge may wish to tell jurors to report to the judge if anyone reads their notes out loud or quotes from their notes during deliberations. *Jurors must be reminded of the errors of reporting that may be in anyone's notes.* It takes a lot of

STRUCTURES THAT INFLUENCE THINKING

ABA Jury Principle	Jury Thinking
	training and certification to become a court reporter. *Voir Dire*: If jurors are going to be allowed to take notes, ask them what value they place on note-taking and what dangers it holds. How will a juror feel if they decide not to take notes but others do? How will they feel if someone says "It was in my notes!"? What will they miss when taking notes? Alert them to the issues, before note-taking happens, and see what their juror thinking is on note-taking during testimony. Find out who knows shorthand. The safest practice based upon group dynamics, status, and memory failures reported in PRACTICAL JURY DYNAMICS would be the simple request that notes are kept outside the courtroom. If a juror wishes to view their notes, the only legitimate reason is for personal memory enhancement, and a break can be had to accomplish that.
Principle 13(C): In civil cases, jurors should, ordinarily, be permitted to **submit written questions** for witnesses ... in criminal cases the court should take into consideration the historic reasons why courts in a number of jurisdictions have discouraged juror questions and the experience in those jurisdictions that have allowed it.	That this is dangerous is obvious and the historical reason for allowing it was not based on hard science: jurors would be more satisfied with their jury service and feel more involved. Clearly, one danger is that we switch from a 3 part system (judge, attorneys, jury) to a system where jurors get to be jury sometimes and advocate others. Why not let them have a go at the bench? When a juror becomes an advocate (wanting something proven or discredited is an advocacy task), one party is faced with impeaching or cross-examining

JURY THINKING

ABA Jury Principle	Jury Thinking
	that juror's "new" answers. No one has yet explained how to avoid this. While the rule impinges on clients' rights, this book takes a Juror's Task as the focal point. Here, the problem is that group status can result from having one's question "accepted" and distracting disappointment or embarrassment when one's question was "denied." Who got the most questions asked? What affects flow during deliberations? The true test should be the "open mind" test: no juror should be allowed to ask any question that impeaches any witness or fact, that bolsters any witness or fact, or that fills in a gap that would have benefited one of the parties. A juror can merely indicate a personal confusion, and the parties can decide what, if anything, to do about that.
Principle 13(F): Jurors in civil cases may be instructed that they will be permitted to discuss the evidence among themselves in the jury room during recesses from the trial when all are present, as long as they reserve judgment about the outcome of the case until deliberations commence.	Since studies of juries using this rule found clearly that many juries violated the "reserve" judgment rules, as well as the "talk only when all are present rule" it is surprising this Principle survived. Get a copy of the 2003 study by Diamond and her colleagues, proving the number of violations.[68]
Principle 13(G): Parties and courts should be open to a variety of trial techniques to enhance juror comprehension of the issues ...	Authority for all attempts to create more democratic juries previously discussed, including seat arrangements, tables, and juror-centered breaks and trial schedules.

STRUCTURES THAT INFLUENCE THINKING

ABA Jury Principle	Jury Thinking
Principle 15: Courts and parties have a duty to facilitate effective and impartial deliberations	
Principle 15(B): Exhibits admitted into evidence should ordinarily be provided to the jury for use during deliberations ...	This skews jury deliberations, over-valuing and attending to physical exhibits, to the marginalization of trial testimony (oral) which jurors are expected to remember. **JURY THINKING** encourages attention to the obvious results of this rule: each juror will have a memory burden/deficit for oral testimony and a memory aid for exhibits. The principles of evidence make it clear that no piece of evidence or form of evidence should be valued over another. Principle 15(B) should be objected to, if suggested. If exhibits are allowed into the jury room, the only remedy for a party whose primary case or impeachment was presented in the form of oral testimony is to request to: (a) have a transcript go into the jury room, (b) have a separate reporter record at the party's expense so quick transcripts can be made each day and go into the jury room, or (c) tape record or video record the testimony, so that can go into the jury room. Under 15B physical evidence introduced at trial (easier to remember by all jurors) will, nonetheless, be given to them during deliberations, while fragile evidence (oral testimony) must be remembered (or preserved in uncertified personal juror notes). This is unfair.

ABA Jury Principle	Jury Thinking
	No justification for this rule, under the rules of evidence, can be made. It appears, however, that it has yet to be taken up on appeal. If this is a significant issue, check with an appellate attorney to learn how to make the best possible record on the issue. Consider ways to reduce critical oral testimony to charts, tables, blow ups of prior statements, photos, exhibits, physical objects, and video demonstrations, so that it can be admitted to the juryroom. Finally, the rule suggests a new question topic for voir dire, probing each juror's evaluation of their own memory, over days and weeks, and any prior tasks where they have had to do that.

§ 5-2(b). Reform Structures Missing from the ABA Principles

In PRACTICAL JURY DYNAMICS, the inequality inside a juryroom was described, based upon the shape of the table and seating arrangements. Since then, the ABA Principles for Juries has appeared, yet two major reforms to insure democracy during deliberations are missing. Since the ABA principles (as referenced above) specifically encourage continual innovative thinking and anticipate new reform, three additional innovations are suggested:

STRUCTURES THAT INFLUENCE THINKING

Innovation 1: Mix It Up in the Jury Box

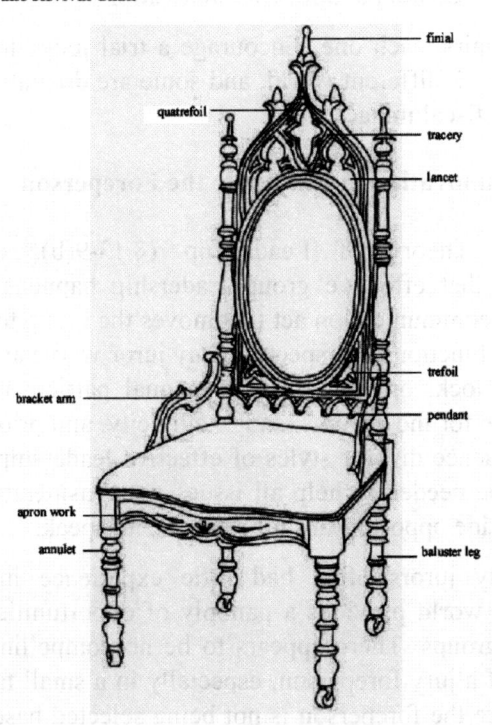

Gothic Revival Chair

Some jury chairs are more equal than others. There is no reason, today, why jurors should sit in the **same seats** in the courtroom all day long, everyday—and there are several reasons that this arrangement impedes justice. *Consider the following practical thoughts abut a juror's world in the courtroom:*

- The trial judge does not need a seating chart to keep track of jurors (desires are different than needs). Jurors can wear badges.

- Some jurors get a better view of the witnesses than others. This is critical for evaluating testimony, demeanor, and noticing important details.

- Jurors begin unconsciously "clumping" with fellow jurors when they take seats next to them; some jurors feel distant from casual talking cliques that develop with rigid seating arrangements.

- Jurors in the back row are less involved and feel less courtroom intensity than jurors in the front row. The proposed ABA trial reforms are designed to increase juror commitment and involvement. Rigid rules about who sits in the back row do not advance trial innovation.

Sit in the jury chairs, each one. Encourage a trial judge to sit in the chairs. Each offers a view of a different world, and some are dramatically unequal. We can fix that, without fiscal impact.

Innovation 2: Eliminate the Foreperson

The Functional Theory of Leadership (§ 13-9(b), PRACTICAL JURY DYNAMICS) argues that effective group leadership happens when *any* group member performs a communication act that moves the group toward accomplishing its task. From a functional perspective, *any* juror who can help lead the jury into or out of deadlock, opinion-jam, or unequal participation is performing functional leadership for the group. Gender, ethnicity, and prior life experiences, to name a few, influence diverse styles of effective leadership, and many styles of leadership may be needed to help all issues get consideration, all jurors feel listened to, and provide opportunities for everyone to speak.

While historically jurors often had little experience in decision-making groups, the modern world provides a panoply of opportunities for everyone to participate in task groups. There appears to be no compelling reason today to force the election of a jury foreperson, especially in a small task group (6 to 12 members), and where the foreperson is not being selected based on a thoughtful consideration of what type of leader will be needed by the group; rarely will a particular jury, in fact, know what type of leader will be needed at the outset of their deliberations. No study to date has demonstrated that a jury would flounder without a foreperson, while many describe the democracy that is lost as a result of this group structure. It's time for change. *Jurors can be encouraged to step up to the leadership plate as often as needed.* Discussions will be the richer for it. Give or request the following instruction:

> YOU ARE INSTRUCTED THAT NO FORMAL LEADER NEED BE SELECTED. A VARIETY OF LEADERSHIP STYLES MAY BENEFIT THIS JURY. ALL JURORS SHOULD SHARE THEIR LEADERSHIP SKILLS THROUGHOUT DELIBERATIONS, IN ORDER TO INSURE THAT ISSUES ARE FAIRLY DISCUSSED, EVIDENCE AND LAW ARE FULLY CONSIDERED, AND ALL JURORS HAVE EQUAL OPPORTUNITIES TO SPEAK AND ARE APPROPRIATELY LISTENED TO.

STRUCTURES THAT INFLUENCE THINKING

Innovation 3: Eliminate the Jury Table

There exists no rational reason for a rectangular table in any juryroom, as the shape of such a table fosters inappropriate juror clumping and unequal visual accessibility during discussions (§ 10-2(b) & (c), PRACTICAL JURY DYNAMICS). While it is tempting to consider arguing on behalf of *King Arthur's Round Table*, such a table would provoke a Goldilock's Dilemma: too large for some juries, too small for others, and only occasionally just right.

In fact, notetaking *during* jury deliberations is not a prime activity, if it exists at all. Eliminating the table would provide immediate equality, as the jurors form a circle of chairs, with equal speaking/listening access to one another. No fiscal impact. (Should a writing surface be deemed essential by any judge, the typical college classroom chair-with-attached-writing-board would suffice.)

The legal system takes for granted the enactment of a democratic process inside the juryroom. Can a "just" trial be had when all jurors do not participate (or participate at such an unequal level that some voices are either unheard or altogether silent), or while some jurors are more equal than others?

```
There is no such thing as an impartial jury, because
there are no impartial people. There are people that ar-
gue on the web for hours about who their favorite char-
acter on Friends is.


                                              —Jon Stewart
```

Chapter 6

IMPERFECT THINKING

寂

The way of Wabi Sabi honors the quirks,
the oddities, the humble,
the unconventional.
All things imperfect,
which is truly *all* things.

–Taro Gold, *Living Wabi Sabi*

Imperfect thinking is continual, confusing, and unavoidable. As a result, *imperfect thinking* is a concept that offers a rich harvest for thinking about a juror's trial task. Imperfect thinking bends reality. One party's success at trial may depend upon effectively revealing the imperfect thinking of someone (or something) else, to imperfect-thinking jurors.

JURY THINKING

§ 6-1. Machine-Thinking

First, it is worth noticing that one party's success at trial may depend upon the "thinking" of a machine. We rely upon machines to live our lives so completely, today, that machines may have become dangerously invisible to us when **machine-thinking** is a key element of our opponent's case at trial: cars, cameras, computers, copiers, coffee-makers, microwaves, cell-phones, automatic teller machines, all drive our professional and personal lives. Consequently, a juror's attention must be effectively drawn to the fallibility of machine-thinking, during voir dire, in cross-examination, in opening statements, to name a few. In effect, when a machine generates information that promises to hurt clients at trial, attorneys want to alert jurors:

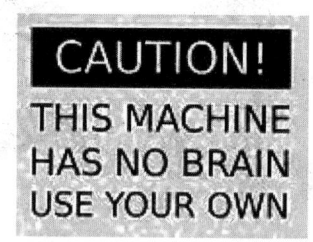

> **CAUTION!**
> THIS MACHINE
> HAS NO BRAIN
> USE YOUR OWN

Any machine's output can be no better than its calibration, maintenance, training of the person giving it input, or skill of the person interpreting its output on any specific day. Attorneys know this, of course, and are skilled at cross-examining on those factors—but a juror's brain needs a succinct, retainable reminder of the persuasive point of such a cross-examination. What is the thinking theme?

> **Practice Tip**: Create a visual tool for the jurors and the witness that will be retained and remembered. Make a large sign like the one above, bright yellow background and black letters (see § 3-1, PRACTICAL JURY DYNAMICS, effects of color perception on recall).
>
> **Attorney:** The machine that ran the test didn't have this sign sitting next to it, did it? [Sign displayed.]
>
> **Witness:** [Smugly] No.
>
> **Attorney:** According to what you know about that machine, however, if the sign had been there, it would be speaking the truth, true?
>
> **Witness**: Of course.

IMPERFECT THINKING

> **Attorney**: That means, then, that the machine was borrowing the brains of people, true?
>
> **Witness**: What do you mean?
>
> **Attorney**: [Traditional cross on calibration, maintenance, input, interpretation.]
>
> **Attorney**: Even human brains that machines borrow are imperfect, though, true? The machine didn't have a brain. It borrowed five of them from other people. True?

All persuasive points in the courtroom benefit from being accompanied by a *succinct thinking theme* for the juror, who is already on *information overload* (§ 6-1, PRACTICAL JURY DYNAMICS, on a juror's mind and the effects of **Information Anxiety**). The **thinking theme** of an attorney's complex cross-examination concerning the output or reliability of some machine is always this:

THAT MACHINE HAD NO BRAIN.

Helping jurors see their own *imperfect thinking* is more challenging, however. A core concept of Japanese culture offers a surprising tool for the courtroom.

§ 6-2. Wabi-Sabi Minds

> Things wabi-sabi are made of materials that are visibly vulnerable to the effect of weathering and human treatment. They record the sun, wind, rain, heat, and cold in a language of discoloration, rust, tarnish, stain, warping, shrinking, shriveling, and cracking. Their nicks, chips, bruises, scars, dents, peeling, and other forms of attribution are a testament to histories of use and misuse.
>
> Leonard Koren[69]

Wabi-sabi has been described as a world view, an aesthetic system, and a move toward the simple life. When asked to explain wabi-sabi, most Japanese will hesitate, then offer an apology about how difficult the concept is to describe.* For most westerners, wabi-sabi is an unfamiliar compass, yet for trial advocates, consultants, and judges, it may be the most underutilized useful tool available. *Trials break regularly*: witnesses do not show up, times are misjudged, tempers flare, exhibits are lost, testimony is changed, rules are broken, admonishments ignored, memories fade, victims are scared, jurors fall ill, wounds are displayed, hearts are broken, and minds are misused. *A courtroom is always a wabi-sabi world.*

Even though things wabi-sabi may be on the point of dematerialization (faint, fragile, desiccated), they are still seen to possess an undiminished poise and strength of character. The Chinese characters used to write wabi-sabi originated three thousand years ago: "wabi" represents the inner spiritual experience, an empty or basic state; "sabi" represents the outer material world, worn, weathered, decayed.[70]

Things wabi-sabi—faded, broken, aging—beckon: get close, touch, relate. These not-perfect-things inspire a reduction of psychic distance between one thing and another, or between people and things. Looking through wabi-sabi eyes, we might see jurors differently. The beauty and value of each juror's imperfect parts, once realized, encourages a humbler acceptance of our own. The trial advocate who accepts a juror's imperfect thinking can offer that juror something that will be, in the end, accepted.

[engage in wabi-sabi thinking here:]

unplug iPod

music stops abruptly

cricket song instead

---

* While *wabi-sabi* is embedded in the Japanese culture, the concept has emerged around the world. In olden times, the finest and most expensive Persian carpets were deliberately *marred* to add texture and allure. Many Navaho weavers leave portions of a pattern *incomplete*, imperfect. Native American sand painters intentionally leave each masterpiece *unfinished*. In the sciences, *imperfect mistakes* have led to the discovery of DNA, penicillin, aspirin, x-rays, nylon, cornflakes, and chocolate chip cookies.

§ 6-3. Thinking in Paradox

Since most of us would often be better off with fewer choices and many of us try too hard to make perfect choices, it follows that juror thinking would improve when a juror is presented with **uncluttered options** reflecting simple values they already embrace. Choosing is stressful, particularly so, when accompanied by paradox.

§ 6-3(a). Unavoidable Paradox

> CHOICE OFFERS, SIMULTANEOUSLY, FREEDOM AND CONSTRAINT.

Choice is a blessing and a burden. There's the paradox. As the number of available choices increases, the autonomy and control this variety brings are powerful and positive; at the same time, as choices grow, the negatives escalate until people become choice-overloaded. **Choice Anxiety** (not unlike Information Anxiety, § 6-1, PRACTICAL JURY DYNAMICS) is a juror thinking reality everyday, in trial and at home.

Jurors know this is true; the everyday world of a juror is full of a ridiculous number of choices they do not need, yet cannot escape: in the grocery store, shopping for a gift, choosing medical care, at the pharmacy, buying a car, selecting a cell phone plan, choosing cable options, locating a repair person, picking a dentist, using the information from web searches, keeping a secret, breaking up with a romantic partner, disclosing information, choosing a credit card, selecting an over-the-counter pain killer (or shampoo!). A juror is constantly thinking about choices. The possibility that a juror may have to serve on a trial is, itself, full of new (unwelcome) choices and forces a **choice-triage**.

Barry Schwartz[71] recently described the ocean of choices that now confront people in every moment of their most ordinary days. The consumer is faced with choice anxiety when shopping for gadgets, shopping by mail, shopping for universities/courses/majors, shopping for entertainment, choosing relationships, to name a few. A juror may have had experience with the anxiety of choosing utilities, retirement plans, investments, medical care, beauty products/procedures (what do you want to look like?). There are a lot of "how" choices as well: how to work, how to love, how to pray. It is worth thinking about what it means to choose and how many choice layers are included in any trial-event of a critical witness.

> **Practice Tip: Reveal and Elaborate a Witness's Choices.**
>
> For a juror to actively think about, relate to, and effectively store information about a witness's choices. This is a longer cross-examination than we generally believe is needed. Highlighting the overwhelming number of choices a witness had at **One Moment in Time**, however, can be the critical theme in a case ("You had choices didn't you?"). The more choices a witness had and continued to have, the more likely a juror will think about that witness as in control and responsible for the outcome (the bad outcome was *avoidable*).

> **Practice Tip: Choices Block Choices for Other People**
>
> Every time an expert, co-worker, witness, police officer, doctor, nurse, mechanic has made a choice, they have constrained the choices for someone else. Think about it.
>
> - Cross-examine a witness on the effect of each and every micro-choice in One Moment of Time on the choices that were taken away from others, as a result.
>
> - Show how reality narrowed for others because of paths not taken by the witness that the witness was aware of. ("But if you had chosen X, then Y would have still been possible for Z.")

§ 6-3(b). Paradox of Choice

In order to engage jurors in meaningful thinking about the choice-dance of another person (client or witness), it is worthwhile to organize the steps to an effective deciding/choosing task:

1. Decide: what do you want as an outcome(s)?
2. Rank all possible outcomes in order of importance.
3. Note conflicting goals or outcomes.
4. Evaluate how likely each of the possible choices you can make will be to help you meet your goal(s).
5. Recall your past experiences (saliency, recency) with each choice and the resulting outcomes that occurred.

IMPERFECT THINKING

6. Recall the past experiences of others of which you are aware.
7. Predict the likely outcomes. Rate the level of confidence you have in your prediction.
8. Choose.
9. Constantly monitor your choice for unexpected variables. Re-choose if possible or necessary.
10. Repeat 7 and 8, as needed.

This list will give you, practically, an outline of how to cross-examine someone else on the choices involved. [To practice, write out all the choices you have to make, just to get out the door in the morning, even those done on automatic pilot.]

You can also cross-examine witnesses on whether they had to do their choosing alone and unaided, or whether they could have had assistance. Choosing unaided, in the modern world, is never by necessity, as myriad experts, friends, cyber-spots, and, yes, even books and articles, are available to help us choose.

Cross-examine the witness on how they gathered information for the choice they made. What was their perception of the quality and of the quantity of information they had before the choice?

Jurors have been thinking about choice all of their lives. It is an area they know a lot about. Putting choice on the table, with its burden and responsibilities is a powerful litigation theme. In every case in which choice is a theme, regret will emerge. The anticipated sting of regret is a legitimate, relevant, and intriguing area for cross-examination. Jurors wonder how other people handle regret—or whether they acknowledge it at all. How, finally, does a witness acknowledge that the anticipated sting of regret colored their decision?

The paradox of choice is its freedom and its tyranny.

A courtroom with jurors is full of paradox—a wonderfully imperfect world.

**Seek always to progress
rather than to perfect.**

American Bar Association

ABA
Defending Liberty
Pursuing Justice

PRINCIPLES FOR JURIES AND JURY TRIALS

American Jury Project

Patricia Lee Refo, Chair

Co-Chairs

Hon. Catherine Anderson, Chair, ABA Criminal Justice Section Hon. Louraine Arkfeld, Chair, ABA Judicial Division Dennis Drasco, Chair, ABA Section of Litigation

Stephan Landsman, Reporter

Members

David Biderman, Pat Brady, Dorothy Brown, Paul Butler, Hon. Charles Clevert, Hon. William Caprathe, Neil Cohen, Mark Curriden, Hon. Michael Dann, Shari Diamond, Neil Ellis, Ken Frazier, Terry MacCarthy, Hon. Greg Mize, Tom Munsterman, Carlos Singh, Dwight Smith

Reprinted from *Principles for Juries & Jury Trials,* American Bar Association, August 2005. Reprinted by permission.

JURY THINKING

PREAMBLE

The American jury is a living institution that has played a crucial part in our democracy for more than two hundred years. The American Bar Association recognizes the legal community's ongoing need to refine and improve jury practice so that the right to jury trial is preserved and juror participation enhanced. What follows is a set of 19 principles that define our fundamental aspirations for the management of the jury system. Each principle is designed to express the best of current-day jury practice in light of existing legal and practical constraints. It is anticipated that over the course of the next decade jury practice will improve so that the principles set forth will have to be updated in a manner that will draw them ever closer to the principles to which we aspire.

PRINCIPLES FOR JURIES AND JURY TRIALS

GENERAL PRINCIPLES

PRINCIPLE 1 – THE RIGHT TO JURY TRIAL SHALL BE PRESERVED

A. Parties in civil matters have the right to a fair, accurate and timely jury trial in accordance with law.

B. Parties, including the state, have the right to a fair, accurate and timely jury trial in criminal prosecutions in which confinement in jail or prison may be imposed.

C. In civil cases the right to jury trial may be waived as provided by applicable law, but waiver should neither be presumed nor required where the interests of justice demand otherwise.

D. With respect to criminal prosecutions:

1. A defendant's waiver of the right to jury trial must be knowing and voluntary, joined in by the prosecutor and accepted by the court.

2. The court should not accept a waiver unless the defendant, after being advised by the court of his or her right to trial by jury and the consequences of waiver, personally waives the right to trial by jury in writing or in open court on the record.

3. A defendant may not withdraw a voluntary and knowing waiver as a matter of right, but the court, in its discretion, may permit withdrawal prior to the commencement of trial.

4. A defendant may withdraw a waiver of jury, and the prosecutor may withdraw its consent to a waiver, both as a matter of right, if there is a change of trial judge.

E. A quality and accessible jury system should be maintained with budget procedures that will ensure adequate, stable, long-term funding under all economic conditions.

PRINCIPLE 2 – CITIZENS HAVE THE RIGHT TO PARTICIPATE IN JURY SERVICE AND THEIR SERVICE SHOULD BE FACILITATED

A. All persons should be eligible for jury service except those who:

1. Are less than eighteen years of age; or

2. Are not citizens of the United States; or

3. Are not residents of the jurisdiction in which they have been summoned to serve; or

4. Are not able to communicate in the English language and the court is unable to provide a satisfactory interpreter; or

5. Have been convicted of a felony and are in actual confinement or on probation, parole or other court supervision.

B. Eligibility for jury service should not be denied or limited on the basis of race, national origin, gender, age, religious belief, income, occupation, disability, sexual orientation, or any other factor that discriminates against a cognizable group in the jurisdiction other than those set forth in A. above.

C. The time required of persons called for jury service should be the shortest period consistent with the needs of justice.

1. Courts should use a term of service of one day or the completion of one trial, whichever is longer.

2. Where deviation from the term of service set forth in C.1. above is deemed necessary, the court should not require a person to remain available to be selected for jury service for longer than two weeks.

D. Courts should respect jurors' time by calling in the minimum number deemed necessary and by minimizing their waiting time.

1. Courts should coordinate jury management and calendar management to make effective use of jurors.

2. Courts should determine the minimally sufficient number of jurors needed to accommodate trial activity. This information and appropriate management techniques should be used to adjust both the number of persons summoned for jury duty and the number assigned to jury panels.

3. Courts should ensure that all jurors in the courthouse waiting to be assigned to panels for the first time are assigned before any juror is assigned a second time.

E. Courts should provide an adequate and suitable environment for jurors, including those who require reasonable accommodation due to disability.

F. Persons called for jury service should receive a reasonable fee.

1. Persons called for jury service should be paid a reasonable fee that will, at a minimum, defray routine expenses such as travel,

parking, meals and child-care. Courts should be encouraged to increase the amount of the fee for persons serving on lengthy trials.

2. Employers should be prohibited from discharging, laying off, denying advancement opportunities to, or otherwise penalizing employees who miss work because of jury service.

3. Employers should be prohibited from requiring jurors to use leave or vacation time for the time spent on jury service or be required to make up the time they served.

PRINCIPLE 3 – JURIES SHOULD HAVE 12 MEMBERS

A. Juries in civil cases should be constituted of 12 members wherever feasible and under no circumstances fewer than six members.

B. Juries in criminal cases should consist of:

1. Twelve persons if a penalty of confinement for more than six months may be imposed upon conviction;

2. At least six persons if the maximum period of confinement that may be imposed upon conviction is six months or less.

C. At any time before verdict, the parties, with the approval of the court, may stipulate that the jury shall consist of fewer jurors than required for a full jury, but in no case fewer than six jurors. In criminal cases the court should not accept such a stipulation unless the defendant, after being advised by the court of his or her right to trial by a full jury, and the consequences of waiver, personally waives the right to a full jury either in writing or in open court on the record.

PRINCIPLE 4 – JURY DECISIONS SHOULD BE UNANIMOUS

A. In civil cases, jury decisions should be unanimous wherever feasible. A less-than-unanimous decision should be accepted only after jurors have deliberated for a reasonable period of time and if concurred in by at least five-sixths of the jurors. In no civil case should a decision concurred in by fewer than six jurors be accepted, except as provided in C. below.

B. A unanimous decision should be required in all criminal cases heard by a jury.

C. At any time before verdict, the parties, with the approval of the court, may stipulate to a less-than-unanimous decision. To be valid, the stipulation should be clear as to the number of concurring jurors required for the verdict. In criminal cases, the court should not accept such a stipulation unless the defendant, after being advised by the court of his or her right to a unanimous decision, personally waives that right, either in writing or in open court on the record.

PRINCIPLE 5 – IT IS THE DUTY OF THE COURTS TO ENFORCE AND PROTECT THE RIGHTS TO JURY TRIAL AND JURY SERVICE

A. The responsibility for administration of the jury system should be vested exclusively in the judicial branch of government.

1. All procedures concerning jury selection and service should be governed by rules and regulations promulgated by the state's highest court or judicial council.

2. A unified jury system should be established wherever feasible in areas that have two or more courts conducting jury trials. This applies whether the courts are of the same or of differing subject matter or geographic jurisdiction.

3. Responsibility for administering the jury system should be vested in a single administrator or clerk acting under the supervision of a presiding judge of the court.

B. Courts should collect and analyze information regarding the performance of the jury system on a regular basis in order to ensure:

1. The representativeness and inclusiveness of the jury source list;

2. The effectiveness of qualification and summoning procedures;

3. The responsiveness of individual citizens to jury duty summonses;

4. The efficient use of jurors; and

5. The reasonableness of accommodations being provided to jurors with disabilities.

PRINCIPLE 6 – COURTS SHOULD EDUCATE JURORS REGARDING THE ESSENTIAL ASPECTS OF A JURY TRIAL

A. Courts should provide orientation and preliminary information to persons called for jury service:

1. Upon initial contact prior to service;

2. Upon first appearance at the courthouse; and

3. Upon reporting to a courtroom for juror voir dire.

B. Orientation programs should be:

1. Designed to increase jurors' understanding of the judicial system and prepare them to serve competently as jurors;

2. Presented in a uniform and efficient manner using a combination of written, oral and audiovisual materials; and

3. Presented, at least in part, by a judge.

C. Throughout the course of the trial, the court should provide instructions to the jury in plain and understandable language.

1. The court should give preliminary instructions directly following empanelment of the jury that explain the jury's role, the trial procedures including note-taking and questioning by jurors, the nature of evidence and its evaluation, the issues to be addressed, and the basic relevant legal principles, including the elements of the charges and claims and definitions of unfamiliar legal terms.

2. The court should advise jurors that once they have been selected to serve as jurors or alternates in a trial, they are under an obligation to refrain from talking about the case outside the jury room until the trial is over and the jury has reached a verdict. At the time of such instructions in civil cases, the court may inform the jurors about the permissibility of discussing the evidence among themselves as contemplated in Standard 13 F.

3. The court should give such instructions during the course of the trial as are necessary to assist the jury in understanding the facts and law of the case being tried as described in Standard 13 D. 2.

4. Prior to deliberations, the court should give such instructions as are described in Standard 14 regarding the applicable law and the conduct of deliberations.

PRINCIPLE 7 – COURTS SHOULD PROTECT JUROR PRIVACY INSOFAR AS CONSISTENT WITH THE REQUIREMENTS OF JUSTICE AND THE PUBLIC INTEREST

A. Juror interest in privacy must be balanced against party and public interest in court proceedings.

1. Juror voir dire should be open and accessible for public view except as provided herein. Closing voir dire proceedings should only occur after a finding by the court that there is a threat to the safety of the jurors or evidence of attempts to intimidate or influence the jury.

2. Requests to jurors for information should differentiate among information collected for the purpose of juror qualification, jury administration, and voir dire.

3. Judges should ensure that jurors' privacy is reasonably protected, and that questioning is consistent with the purpose of the voir dire process.

4. Courts should explain to jurors how the information they provide will be used, how long it will be retained, and who will have access to it.

5. Courts should consider juror privacy concerns when choosing the method of voir dire (open questioning in court, private questioning at the bench, or a jury questionnaire) to be used to inquire about sensitive matters.

6. Courts should inform jurors that they may provide answers to sensitive questions privately to the court, and the parties.

7. Jurors should be examined outside the presence of other jurors with respect to questions of prior exposure to potentially prejudicial material.

8. Following jury selection and trial, the court should keep all jurors' home and business addresses and telephone numbers confidential and under seal unless good cause is shown to the court which would require disclosure. Original records, documents and transcripts relating to juror summoning and jury selection may be destroyed when the time for appeal has passed, or the appeal is complete, whichever is longer, provided that, in criminal proceedings, the court maintains for use by the parties and the public exact replicas (using any reliable process that ensures

their integrity and preservation) of those items and devices for viewing them.

B. Without express court permission, surveillance of jurors and prospective jurors outside the courtroom by or on behalf of a party should be prohibited.

C. If cameras are permitted to be used in the courtroom, they should not be allowed to record or transmit images of the jurors' faces.

PRINCIPLE 8 – INDIVIDUALS SELECTED TO SERVE ON A JURY HAVE AN ONGOING INTEREST IN COMPLETING THEIR SERVICE

During trial and deliberations, a juror should be removed only for a compelling reason. The determination that a juror should be removed should be made by the court, on the record, after an appropriate hearing.

ASSEMBLING A JURY

PRINCIPLE 9 – COURTS SHOULD CONDUCT JURY TRIALS IN THE VENUE REQUIRED BY APPLICABLE LAW OR THE INTERESTS OF JUSTICE

A. In civil cases where a jury demand has been made, a change of venue may be granted as required by applicable law or in the interest of justice.

B. In criminal cases, a change of venue or continuance should be granted whenever there is a substantial likelihood that, in the absence of such relief, a fair trial by an impartial jury cannot be had. A showing of actual prejudice should not be required.

C. Courts should consider the option of trying the case in the original venue but selecting the jury from a new venue. In addition to all other considerations relevant to the selection of the new venue, consideration should be given to whether the original venue would be a better location to conduct the trial due to facilities, security, and the convenience of the victims, court staff, and parties. This should be balanced against the possible inconvenience to the jurors.

PRINCIPLE 10 – COURTS SHOULD USE OPEN, FAIR AND FLEXIBLE PROCEDURES TO SELECT A REPRESENTATIVE POOL OF PROSPECTIVE JURORS

A. Juror source pools should be assembled so as to assure representativeness and inclusiveness.

　　1. The names of potential jurors should be drawn from a jury source list compiled from two or more regularly maintained source lists of persons residing in the jurisdiction. These source lists should be updated at least annually.

　　2. The jury source list and the assembled jury pool should be representative and inclusive of the eligible population in the jurisdiction. The source list and the assembled jury pool are representative of the population to the extent the percentages of cognizable group members on the source list and in the assembled jury pool are reasonably proportionate to the corresponding percentages in the population.

　　3. The court should periodically review the jury source list and the assembled jury pool for their representativeness and inclusiveness of the eligible population in the jurisdiction.

　　4. Should the court determine that improvement is needed in the representativeness or inclusiveness of the jury source list or the assembled jury pool, appropriate corrective action should be taken.

　　5. Jury officials should determine the qualifications of prospective jurors by questionnaire or interview, and disqualify those who fail to meet eligibility requirements.

B. Courts should use random selection procedures throughout the juror selection process.

　　1. Any selection method may be used, manual or automated, that provides each eligible and available person with an equal probability of selection, except when a court orders an adjustment for underrepresented populations.

　　2. Courts should use random selection procedures in:

　　　　a. Selecting persons to be summoned for jury service;

　　　　b. Assigning jurors to panels;

　　　　c. Calling jurors for voir dire; and

PRINCIPLES FOR JURIES AND JURY TRIALS

        d.   Designating, at the outset of jury deliberations, those jurors who will serve as "regular" and as "alternate" jurors.

    3.   Departures from the principle of random selection are appropriate:

        a.   To exclude persons ineligible for service in accordance with basic eligibility requirements;

        b.   To excuse or defer jurors in accordance with C. below;

        c.   To remove jurors for cause or if challenged peremptorily in accordance with D. and E. below; or

        d.   To provide jurors who have not been considered for selection with an opportunity to be considered before other jurors are considered for a second time, as provided for in Standard 2 D. 3.

C.   Exemptions, excuses, and deferrals should be sparingly used.

    1.   All automatic excuses or exemptions from jury service should be eliminated.

    2.   Eligible persons who are summoned may be excused from jury service only if:

        a.   Their ability to perceive and evaluate information is so impaired that even with reasonable accommodations having been provided, they are unable to perform their duties as jurors and they are excused for this reason by a judge; or

        b.   Their service would be an undue hardship or they have served on a jury during the two years preceding their summons and they are excused by a judge or duly authorized court official.

    3.   Deferrals of jury service to a date certain within six months should be permitted by a judge or duly authorized court official. Prospective jurors seeking to postpone their jury service to a specific date should be permitted to submit a request by telephone, mail, in person or electronically. Deferrals should be preferred to excusals whenever possible.

    4.   Requests for excuses or deferrals and their disposition should be written or otherwise made of record. Specific uniform guide-

lines for determining such requests should be adopted by the court.

D. Courts should use sensible and practical notification and summons procedures in assembling jurors.

1. The notice summoning a person to jury service should be easy to understand and answer, should specify the steps required for answering and the consequences of failing to answer, should allow for speedy and accurate eligibility screening, and should request basic background information.

2. Courts should adopt specific uniform guidelines for enforcing a summons for jury service and for monitoring failures to respond to a summons. Courts should utilize appropriate sanctions in the cases of persons who fail to respond to a jury summons.

E. Opportunity to challenge the assembled jury pool should be afforded all parties on the ground that there has been material departure from the requirements of the law governing selection of jurors. The court should maintain demographic information as to its source lists, summonses issued, and reporting jurors.

PRINCIPLE 11 – COURTS SHOULD ENSURE THAT THE PROCESS USED TO EMPANEL JURORS EFFECTIVELY SERVES THE GOAL OF ASSEMBLING A FAIR AND IMPARTIAL JURY

A. Before voir dire begins, the court and parties, through the use of appropriate questionnaires, should be provided with data pertinent to the eligibility of jurors and to matters ordinarily raised in voir dire, including such background information as is provided by prospective jurors in their responses to the questions appended to the notification and summons considered in Standard 10 D. 1.

1. In appropriate cases, the court should consider using a specialized questionnaire addressing particular issues that may arise. The court should permit the parties to submit a proposed juror questionnaire. The parties should be required to confer on the form and content of the questionnaire. If the parties cannot agree, each party should be afforded the opportunity to submit a proposed questionnaire and to comment upon any proposal submitted by another party.

2. Jurors should be advised of the purpose of any questionnaire, how it will be used and who will have access to the information.

3. All completed questionnaires should be provided to the parties in sufficient time before the start of voir dire to enable the parties to adequately review them before the start of that examination.

B. The voir dire process should be held on the record and appropriate demographic data collected.

1. Questioning of jurors should be conducted initially by the court, and should be sufficient, at a minimum, to determine the jurors' legal qualification to serve in the case.

2. Following initial questioning by the court, each party should have the opportunity, under the supervision of the court and subject to reasonable time limits, to question jurors directly, both individually and as a panel. In a civil case involving multiple parties, the court should permit each separately represented party to participate meaningfully in questioning prospective jurors, subject to reasonable time limits and avoidance of repetition.

3. Voir dire should be sufficient to disclose grounds for challenges for cause and to facilitate intelligent exercise of peremptory challenges.

4. Where there is reason to believe that jurors have been previously exposed to information about the case, or for other reasons are likely to have preconceptions concerning it, the parties should be given liberal opportunity to question jurors individually about the existence and extent of their knowledge and preconceptions.

5. It is the responsibility of the court to prevent abuse of the juror selection examination process.

C. Challenges for cause should be available at the request of a party or at the court's own initiative.

1. Each jurisdiction should establish, by law, the grounds for and the standards by which a challenge for cause to a juror is sustained by the court.

2. At a minimum, a challenge for cause to a juror should be sustained if the juror has an interest in the outcome of the case, may be biased for or against one of the parties, is not qualified by law

to serve on a jury, has a familial relation to a participant in the trial, or may be unable or unwilling to hear the subject case fairly and impartially. There should be no limit to the number of challenges for cause.

3. In ruling on a challenge for cause, the court should evaluate the juror's demeanor and substantive responses to questions. If the court determines that there is a reasonable doubt that the juror can be fair and impartial, then the court should excuse him or her from the trial. The court should make a record of the reasons for the ruling including whatever factual findings are appropriate.

D. Peremptory challenges should be available to each of the parties.

1. In the courts of each state, the number of and procedure for exercising peremptory challenges should be uniform.

2. The number of peremptory challenges should be sufficient, but limited to a number no larger than necessary to provide reasonable assurance of obtaining an unbiased jury, and to provide the parties confidence in the fairness of the jury.

3. The court should have the authority to allow additional peremptory challenges when justified.

4. Following completion of the examination of jurors, the parties should exercise their peremptory challenges by alternately striking names from the list of panel members until each side has exhausted or waived the permitted number of challenges.

E. Fair procedures should be utilized in the exercise of challenges.

1. All challenges, whether for cause or peremptory, should be exercised so that the jury panel is not aware of the nature of the challenge, the party making the challenge, or the basis of the court's ruling on the challenge.

2. After completion of the examination of jurors and the hearing and determination of all challenges for cause, the parties should be permitted to exercise their peremptory challenges as set forth in D. 4. above. A party should be permitted to exercise a peremptory challenge against a member of the panel who has been passed for cause.

3. The court should not require a party to exercise any challenges until the attorney for that party has had sufficient time to consult

with the client, and in cases with multiple parties on a side, with co-parties, regarding the exercise of challenges.

4. No juror should be sworn to try the case until all challenges have been exercised or waived, at which point all jurors should be sworn as a group.

F. No party should be permitted to use peremptory challenges to dismiss a juror for constitutionally impermissible reasons.

1. It should be presumed that each party is utilizing peremptory challenges validly, without basing those challenges on constitutionally impermissible reasons.

2. A party objecting to the challenge of a juror on the grounds that the challenge has been exercised on a constitutionally impermissible basis, establishes a prima facie case of purposeful discrimination by showing that the challenge was exercised against a member of a constitutionally cognizable group; and by demonstrating that this fact, and any other relevant circumstances, raise an inference that the party challenged the juror because of the juror's membership in that group.

3. When a prima facie case of discrimination is established, the burden shifts to the party making the challenge to show a nondiscriminatory basis for the challenge.

4. The court should evaluate the credibility of the reasons proffered by the party as a basis for the challenge. If the court finds that the reasons stated are not pretextual and otherwise constitutionally permissible and are supported by the record, the court should permit the challenge. If the court finds that the reasons for the challenge are pretextual, or otherwise constitutionally impermissible, the court should deny the challenge and, after consultation with counsel, determine whether further remedy is appropriate. The court should state on the record the reasons, including whatever factual findings are appropriate, for sustaining or overruling the challenge.

5. When circumstances suggest that a peremptory challenge was used in a constitutionally impermissible manner, the court on its own initiative, if necessary, shall advise the parties on the record of its belief that the challenge is impermissible, and its reasons for so concluding and shall require the party exercising the challenge to make a showing under F. 3. above.

G. The court may empanel a sufficient number of jurors to allow for one or more alternates whenever, in the court's discretion, the court believes it advisable to have such jurors available to replace jurors who, prior to the time the jury retires to consider its verdict, become or are found to be unable or disqualified to perform their duties.

   1. Alternate jurors shall be selected in the same manner, have the same qualifications, be subject to the same examination and challenges, and take the same oath as regular jurors.

   2. The status of jurors as regular jurors or as alternates should be determined through random selection at the time for jury deliberation.

   3. In civil cases where there are 12 or fewer jurors, all jurors, including alternates, should deliberate and vote, but in no case should more than 12 jurors deliberate and vote.

H. Courts should limit the use of anonymous juries to compelling circumstances, such as when the safety of the jurors is an issue or when there is a finding by the court that efforts are being made to intimidate or influence the jury's decision.

CONDUCTING A JURY TRIAL

PRINCIPLE 12 – COURTS SHOULD LIMIT THE LENGTH OF JURY TRIALS INSOFAR AS JUSTICE ALLOWS AND JURORS SHOULD BE FULLY INFORMED OF THE TRIAL SCHEDULE ESTABLISHED

A. The court, after conferring with the parties, should impose and enforce reasonable time limits on the trial or portions thereof.

B. Trial judges should use modern trial management techniques that eliminate unnecessary trial delay and disruption. Once begun, jury trial proceedings with jurors present should take precedence over all other court proceedings except those given priority by a specific law and those of an emergency nature.

C. Jurors should be informed of the trial schedule and of any necessary changes to the trial schedule at the earliest practicable time.

PRINCIPLE 13 – THE COURT AND PARTIES SHOULD VIGOROUSLY PROMOTE JUROR UNDERSTANDING OF THE FACTS AND THE LAW

A. Jurors should be allowed to take notes during the trial.

    1. Jurors should be instructed at the beginning of the trial that they are permitted, but not required, to take notes in aid of their memory of the evidence and should receive appropriate cautionary instructions on note-taking and note use. Jurors should also be instructed that after they have reached their verdict, all juror notes will be collected and destroyed.

    2. Jurors should ordinarily be permitted to use their notes throughout the trial and during deliberations.

    3. The court should ensure that jurors have implements for taking notes.

    4. The court should collect all juror notes at the end of each trial day until the jury retires to deliberate.

    5. After the jurors have returned their verdict, all juror notes should be collected and destroyed.

B. Jurors should, in appropriate cases, be supplied with identical trial notebooks which may include such items as the court's preliminary instructions, selected exhibits which have been ruled admissible, stipulations of the parties and other relevant materials not subject to genuine dispute.

    1. At the time of distribution, the court should instruct the jurors concerning the purpose and use of their trial notebooks.

    2. During the trial, the court may permit the parties to supplement the materials contained in the notebooks with additional material that has been admitted in evidence.

    3. The trial notebooks should be available to jurors during deliberations as well as during the trial.

C. In civil cases, jurors should, ordinarily, be permitted to submit written questions for witnesses. In deciding whether to permit jurors to submit written questions in criminal cases, the court should take into consideration the historic reasons why courts in a number of jurisdictions have discouraged juror questions and the experience in those jurisdictions that have allowed it.

JURY THINKING

1. Jurors should be instructed at the beginning of the trial concerning their ability to submit written questions for witnesses.

2. Upon receipt of a written question, the court should make it part of the court record and disclose it to the parties outside the hearing of the jury. The parties should be given the opportunity, outside the hearing of the jury, to interpose objections and suggest modifications to the question.

3. After ruling that a question is appropriate, the court may pose the question to the witness, or permit a party to do so, at that time or later; in so deciding, the court should consider whether the parties prefer to ask, or to have the court ask, the question. The court should modify the question to eliminate any objectionable material.

4. After the question is answered, the parties should be given an opportunity to ask follow-up questions.

D. The court should assist jurors where appropriate.

1. The court should not in any way indicate to the jury its personal opinion as to the facts or value of evidence by the court's rulings, conduct, or remarks during the trial.

2. When necessary to the jurors' proper understanding of the proceedings, the court may intervene during the taking of evidence to instruct on a principle of law or the applicability of the evidence to the issues. This should be done only when the jurors cannot be effectively advised by postponing the explanation to the time of giving final instructions.

3. The court should exercise self-restraint and preserve an atmosphere of impartiality and detachment, but may question a witness if necessary to assist the jury.

    a. Generally, the court should not question a witness about subject matter not raised by any party with that witness, unless the court has provided the parties an opportunity, outside the hearing of the jury, to explain the omission. If the court believes the questioning is necessary, the court should afford the parties an opportunity to develop the subject by further examination prior to its questioning of the witness.

    b. The court should instruct the jury that questions from the court, like questions from the parties, are not evidence; that only answers are evidence; that questions by the court should not be given special weight or emphasis; and the fact that the court asks a question does not reflect a view on the merits of the case or on the credibility of any witness.

E. The court should control communications with jurors during trial.

   1. The court should take appropriate steps ranging from admonishing the jurors to, in the rarest of circumstances, sequestration of them during trial, to ensure that the jurors will not be exposed to sources of information or opinion, or subject to influences, which might tend to affect their ability to render an impartial verdict on the evidence presented in court.

   2. At the outset of the case, the court should instruct the jury on the relationship between the court, the parties and the jury, ensuring that the jury understands that the parties are permitted to communicate with jurors only in open court with the opposing parties present.

   3. All communications between the judge and members of the jury panel from the time of reporting to the courtroom for juror selection examination until dismissal should be in writing or on the record in open court. Each party should be informed of such communications and given the opportunity to be heard.

F. Jurors in civil cases may be instructed that they will be permitted to discuss the evidence among themselves in the jury room during recesses from trial when all are present, as long as they reserve judgment about the outcome of the case until deliberations commence.

G. Parties and courts should be open to a variety of trial techniques to enhance juror comprehension of the issues including: alteration of the sequencing of expert witness testimony, mini- or interim openings and closings, and the use of computer simulations, deposition summaries and other aids.

H. In civil cases the court should seek a single, unitary trial of all issues in dispute before the same jury, unless bifurcation or severance of issues or parties is required by law or is necessary to prevent unfairness or prejudice.

I. Consistent with applicable rules of evidence and procedure, courts should encourage the presentation of live testimony.

J. The court may empanel two or more juries for cases involving multiple parties, defendants, or claims arising out of the same transaction or cause of action, in order to reduce the number and complexity of issues that any one jury must decide. Dual juries also may be used in order to promote judicial economy by presenting otherwise duplicative evidence in a single trial.

JURY DELIBERATIONS

PRINCIPLE 14 – THE COURT SHOULD INSTRUCT THE JURY IN PLAIN AND UNDERSTANDABLE LANGUAGE REGARDING THE APPLICABLE LAW AND THE CONDUCT OF DELIBERATIONS

A. All instructions to the jury should be in plain and understandable language.

B. Jurors should be instructed with respect to the applicable law before or after the parties' final argument. Each juror should be provided with a written copy of instructions for use while the jury is being instructed and during deliberations.

C. Instructions for reporting the results of deliberations should be given following final argument in all cases. At that time, the court should also provide the jury with appropriate suggestions regarding the process of selecting a presiding juror and the conduct of its deliberations.

D. The jurors alone should select the foreperson and determine how to conduct jury deliberations.

PRINCIPLE 15 – COURTS AND PARTIES HAVE A DUTY TO FACILITATE EFFECTIVE AND IMPARTIAL DELIBERATIONS

A. In civil cases of appropriate complexity, and after consultation with the parties, the court should consider the desirability of a special verdict form tailored to the issues in the case. If the parties cannot agree on a special verdict form, each party should be afforded the opportunity to propose a form and to comment upon any proposal submitted by another party or fashioned by the court. The court should consider furnishing each juror with a copy of the verdict form when the jury is instructed and explaining the form as necessary.

PRINCIPLES FOR JURIES AND JURY TRIALS

B. Exhibits admitted into evidence should ordinarily be provided to the jury for use during deliberations. Jurors should be provided an exhibit index to facilitate their review and consideration of documentary evidence.

C. Jury deliberations should take place under conditions and pursuant to procedures that are designed to ensure impartiality and to enhance rational decision-making.

    1. The court should instruct the jury on the appropriate method for asking questions during deliberations and reporting the results of its deliberations.

    2. A jury should not be required to deliberate after normal working hours unless the court after consultation with the parties and the jurors determines that evening or weekend deliberations would not impose an undue hardship upon the jurors and are required in the interest of justice.

D. When jurors submit a question during deliberations, the court, in consultation with the parties, should supply a prompt, complete and responsive answer or should explain to the jurors why it cannot do so.

E. A jury should be sequestered during deliberations only in the rarest of circumstances and only for the purposes of protecting the jury from threatened harm or insulating its members from improper information or influences.

F. When a verdict has been returned and before the jury has dispersed, the jury should be polled at the request of any party or upon the court's own motion. The poll should be conducted by the court or clerk of court asking each juror individually whether the verdict announced is his or her verdict. If the poll discloses that there is not that level of concurrence required by applicable law, the jury may be directed to retire for further deliberations or may be discharged.

PRINCIPLE 16 – DELIBERATING JURORS SHOULD BE OFFERED ASSISTANCE WHEN AN APPARENT IMPASSE IS REPORTED

A. If the jury advises the court that it has reached an impasse in its deliberations, the court may, after consultation with the parties, inquiry the jurors in writing to determine whether and how court and the parties can assist them in their deliberative process. After receiving the jurors' response, if any, and consulting with the parties, the judge may direct that further proceedings occur as appropriate.

B. If it appears to the court that the jury has been unable to agree, the court may require the jury to continue its deliberations. The court should not require or threaten to require the jury to deliberate for an unreasonable length of time or for unreasonable intervals.

C. If there is no reasonable probability of agreement, the jury may be discharged.

POST-VERDICT ACTIVITY

PRINCIPLE 17 – TRIAL AND APPELLATE COURTS SHOULD AFFORD JURY DECISIONS THE GREATEST DEFERENCE CONSISTENT WITH LAW

Trial and appellate courts should afford jury decisions the greatest deference consistent with law.

PRINCIPLE 18 – COURTS SHOULD GIVE JURORS LEGALLY PERMISSIBLE POST-VERDICT ADVICE AND INFORMATION

A. After the conclusion of the trial and the completion of the jurors' service, the court is encouraged to engage in discussions with the jurors. Such discussions should occur on the record and in open court with the parties having the opportunity to be present, unless all the parties agree to the court conducting these discussions differently. This standard does not prohibit incidental contact between the court and jurors after the conclusion of the trial.

B. Under no circumstances should the court praise or criticize the verdict or state or imply an opinion on the merits of the case, or make any other statements that might prejudice a juror in future jury service.

C. At the conclusion of the trial, the court should instruct the jurors that they have the right either to discuss or to refuse to discuss the case with anyone, including counsel or members of the press.

D. Unless prohibited by law, the court should ordinarily permit the parties to contact jurors after their terms of jury service have expired, subject, in the court's discretion, to reasonable restrictions.

PRINCIPLES FOR JURIES AND JURY TRIALS

E. Courts should inform jurors that they may ask for the assistance of the court in the event that individuals persist in questioning jurors, over their objection, about their jury service.

PRINCIPLE 19 – APPROPRIATE INQUIRIES INTO ALLEGATIONS OF JUROR MISCONDUCT SHOULD BE PROMPTLY UNDERTAKEN BY THE TRIAL COURT

A. Only under exceptional circumstances may a verdict be impeached upon information provided by jurors.

1. Upon an inquiry into the validity of a verdict, no evidence should be received to show the effect of any statement, conduct, event, or condition upon the mind of a juror or concerning the mental processes by which the verdict was determined.

2. The limitations in A.1 above should not bar evidence concerning whether the verdict was reached by lot or contains a clerical error, or was otherwise unlawfully decided.

3. A juror's testimony or affidavit may be received when it concerns:

    a. Whether matters not in evidence came to the attention of one or more jurors; or

    b. Any other misconduct for which the jurisdiction permits jurors to impeach their verdict.

B. The court should take prompt action in response to an allegation of juror misconduct.

1. Upon receipt of an allegation of juror misconduct, the court should promptly inform the parties and afford them the opportunity to be heard as to whether the allegation warrants further enquiry or other judicial action.

2. Parties should promptly refer an allegation of juror misconduct to the court and to all other parties in the proceeding.

3. If the court determines that the allegation of juror misconduct warrants further inquiry, it should consult with the parties concerning the nature and scope of the inquiry, including:

    a. Which jurors should be questioned;

    b. Whether the court or the parties should ask the questions; and

c. The substance of the questions.

4. If the court ascertains that juror misconduct has occurred, it should afford the parties the opportunity to be heard as to an appropriate remedy.

5. If the allegation of juror misconduct is received while the jury is deliberating, the recipient must ensure as quickly as possible that the court and counsel are informed of it, and the court should proceed as promptly as practicable to ascertain the facts and to fashion an appropriate remedy.

BOOKS THAT STIMULATE MINDFUL JURY-THINKING

BROWSE THE STACKS

Ackerman, Diane (2004). *An Alchemy of Mind: The Marvel and Mystery of the Brain.* New York: Scribner.

Ball, David (2005). *David Ball on Damages: A Plaintiff's Attorney's Guide for Personal Injury and Wrongful Death Cases.* National Institute for Trial Advocacy.

Barletta, Martha (2003). *Marketing to Women: How to Understand, Reach, and Increase Your Share of the World's Largest Market Segment.* Chicago, IL: Dearborn Trade Publishing.

Edelman, Gerald M. [winner of the Nobel Prize] (2004). *Wider than the Sky: The Phenomenal Gift of Consciousness.* New Haven: Yale University Press.

Gardner, Howard (2004). *Changing Minds: The Art and Science of Changing Our Own and Other People's Minds.* Boston, MA: Harvard Business School Press.

Gladwell, Malcolm (2005). *Blink: The Power of Thinking Without Thinking.* New York: Little, Brown, & Company.

Gold, Taro (2004). *Living Wabi Sabi: The True Beauty of Your Life.* Kansas City, MO: Andrews McMeel Publishing.

Johnson, Steven (2004). *Mind Wide Open: Your Brain and the Neuroscience of Everyday Life.* New York: Scribner.

Koren, Leonard (1994). *Wabi-Sabi for Artists, Designers, Poets, and Philosophers.* Berkeley, CA: Stone Bridge Press.

Lipton, Bruce (2005). *The Biology of Belief: Unleashing the Power of Consciousness, Matter, and Miracles.* Santa Rosa, CA: Elite Books.

I enthusiastically browse all book stacks (dusty or virtual) and have, consequently, amassed a thick forest of biblio-companions. Works from cognition, social psychology, folklore, neuropsychology, human development, persuasion, group dynamics, marketing, relationships, conflict, philosophy, spirituality, sociology, and literature have profoundly influenced my thinking about jurors. This book list offers a sampling from my own biblio-forest (and supplements an extensive book list previously provided in PRACTICAL JURY DYNAMICS). If you are time-starved (therefore unable to rush to a university library), browse these titles here. Then *listen* to your own intuition about which ones you need to find and to read.

Ortony, Andrew (Ed.) (1993). *Metaphor and Thought* (2nd ed.). Cambridge University Press: New York.

Powell, Richard R. (2005). *Wabi Sabi Simple*. Avon, MA: Adams Media.

Roese, Neal (2005). *If Only: How to Turn Regret into Opportunity*. New York: Broadway Books.

Schwartz, Barry (2004). *The Paradox of Choice: Why More Is Less*. New York: HarperCollins.

ENDNOTES

1. Jaynes, Julian (1990). *The Origin of Consciousness in the Breakdown of the Bicameral Mind.* Boston: Houghton Mifflin.

2. Ackerman, Diane (2004). *An Alchemy of Mind: The Marvel and Mystery of the Brain.* New York: Scribner [p. 41].

3. Calling its product the "Brain inside the Box," TiVo® is the registered trademark for both a television service and a box that automatically finds and digitally records up to 140 hours of programming all while we're out living life—with features that include pause, rewind, and slo-mo live TV; www.tivo.com.

4. Inspired, twisted, and adapted from one of my favorite thinkers about the challenges and illogic of everyday living, Martha Beck, who is the author of *Leaving the Saints*, *The Joy Diet*, and *Finding Your Own North Star*.

5. Barry Schwartz (2004). *The Paradox of Choice: Why More Is Less.* New York: HarperCollins (p. 39).

6. Gregory M. Ashley (2002). Theology in the Jury Room: Religious Discussion as "Extraneous material" in the Course of Capital Punishment Deliberations. 55 *Vand. L. Rev.* 127.

7. *Jones v. Kemp*, 706 F. Supp. 1534 (N.D. Ga. 1989), where jurors' request to the court to use a bible during sentencing deliberations had been granted and was subsequently held to be error.

8. *Jones v. Francis*, 312 S.E.2d 300 (Ga.), where the trial judge permitted the jury to consult the Bible during capital punishment deliberations, but it was held harmless error (although the jury voted for death). See also, for the importance of raising the issue during trial, *James v. Commonwealth*, 247 Va. 459, 442 S.E.2d 396 (1994), upholding a prosecutor's excusal of a black juror for the stated reason that he was wearing a visible religious symbol (cross) when the objection was not raised at trial.

9. Gerald F. Uelmen is Professor of Law at Santa Clara University School of Law, was former dean of the law school, a member of the defense team in People v. O. J. Simpson, and is now Director of the Edwin A. Heafey Jr. Center for Trial and Appellate Advocacy. His 2005 article on Catholic jurors appears in the *Journal of Catholic Legal Studies, 44(2)*.

10. Catechism of the Catholic Church, Paragraph 2267. See also the decades-old U. S. Catholic Bishops' Statement on Capital Punishment, approved November 1980, calling for the abolition of death penalty laws (but not going so far as to suggest that the death penalty is never appropriate).

11. *Witherspoon v. Illinois*, 391 U.S. 510, 88 S.Ct. 1770, 20 L.Ed.2d 776 (1968), *n. 9,* holding, "In trials for murder it shall be a cause for challenge of any juror who shall, on being examined, state that he has conscientious scruples against capital punishment, or that he is opposed to the same."

12. *State v. Davis*, 504 N.W.2d 767 (1993).

13. *Casarez v. State*, 913 S.W.2d 468 (1995).

14. *State v. Fuller*, 356 N.J. Super. 266, 812 A.2d 389 (2002), in which merely dressing as a member of the Muslim faith was viewed as sufficient reason for a peremptory challenge.

15. Data from the NSRI and ARIS data. National Survey of Religious Identification (NSRI) was done in 1990, involving a nationwide survey of 113,000 Americans who were asked about religious preference. The American Religious Identity Survey (ARIS) was conducted in 2001, with a sample size of 50,000 Americans. The ARIS data is published online at www.gc.cuny.edu/studies/aris_index.htm

16. Adapted and significantly expanded from a wonderful issue September 5, 2005, of *Newsweek*: "Spirituality in America: Our Faith Today, What We Believe, How We Pray, Where We Find God."

17. Johnson, Steven (2004). *Mind Wide Open: Your Brain and the Neuroscience of Everyday Life*. New York: Scribner.

18. Ackerman, Diane (2004). *An Alchemy of Mind: The Marvel and Mystery of the Brain*. New York: Scribner [p. 3].

19. Gladwell, Malcolm (2005). *Blink: The Power of Thinking without Thinking*. New York: Little, Brown & Company.

20. Gladwell, Malcolm (2005). *Blink: The Power of Thinking without Thinking*. New York: Little, Brown & Company. This book will make you see other people and yourself in a different way as he revolutionizes the way we understand our inner thinking worlds. How do our brains really work, in the office, in the courtroom, during interviews, in meetings, on the street—and why are some of our best decisions often those that we cannot explain to others?

21. On the damaging effects of trying to put thoughts into words, see, Jonathan W. Schooler, Stellan Ohlsson, and Kevin Brooks, 1993, "Thoughts Beyond Words: When Language Overshadows Insight," *Journal of Experimental Psychology, 122(2)*, 166-183. Criminal defense attorneys will also find this study of use: Chad S. Dodson, Marcia K. Johnson, and Jonathan W. Schooler, 1997, "The Verbal Overshadowing Effect: Why Descriptions Impair Face Recognition," *Memory & Cognition, 25(2)*, 129-139.

22. Gladwell, Malcolm (2005). *Blink: The Power of Thinking without Thinking*. New York: Little, Brown & Company (p. 64). This clarity-to-confusion outcome of forced explaining, however, has been well-documented. See also, the 1977 work of Richard E. Nisbett and Timothy D. Wilson, "Telling more than we can know: Verbal reports on mental processes," *Psychological Review, 84(3)*, 231-259.

ENDNOTES

23. On the issue of doctor malpractice lawsuits, see "How Plaintiffs' Lawyers Pick Their Targets," in *Medical Economics* (April 24, 2000). Also, "Physician-Patient Communication: The Relationship with Malpractice Claims Among Primary Care Physicians and Surgeons," a 1997 article by Wendy Levinson and her colleagues in *Journal of the American Medical Association*, 277(7), 553-559; or, more recently, Nalini Ambady, 2002, "Surgeons' Tone of Voice: A Clue to Malpractice History," *Surgery*, 132(1), 4-9.

24. In *Blink*, Malcolm Gladwell reports the research of Wendy Levinson, who recorded hundreds of conversations between physicians and patients. Half the doctors had never been sued, while the other half had been sued at least twice. Levinson found that just listening to the physician-patient conversations produced such clear differences between the two groups that a subsequent psychologist examining the tapes was able to distinguish the doctors based on *thin-slicing* (using only ten-second clips of talk). Differences appeared in orienting comments, active listening, proding, use of humor, and sharing of more quality information with the patient (*Blink*, pp. 40-44). Subsequent analysis showed tone of voice and dominance (as opposed to "concerned") predicted being in the sued group. In fact, the most corrosive tone of voice a doctor can assume is a dominant tone.

25. Reported in: Gladwell, Malcolm (2005). *Blink: The Power of Thinking without Thinking*. New York: Little, Brown & Company (p. 44).

26. Primary researchers are Anthony G. Greenwald, Nahzarin Banaji, and Brian Nosek. To read more on the IAT, see Anthony G. Greenwald, Debbie E. McGhee, and Jordan L. K. Schwartz (1998). Measuring individual differences in implicit cognition: The Implicit Association Test. *Journal of Personality and Social Psychology, 74(6)*, 1464-1480.

27. Gladwell, Malcolm (2005). *Blink: The Power of Thinking without Thinking*. New York: Little, Brown & Company (pp. 81-82).

28. It turns out that of the 50,000 African Americans who have taken the Race IAT, half, like Malcolm Gladwell, have stronger associations with whites than with blacks. Living in the United States, people are surrounded by cultural messages blinking white with good. "You don't choose to make positive associations with the dominant group, but you are required to. All around you, that group is being paired with good things. You open the newspaper and you turn on the television, and you can't escape it," explained Mahzarin Banaji, who teaches psychology at Harvard University and is one of the leaders in IAT research.

29. Nilanjana Dasgupta & Anthony G. Greenwald (2001). On the malleability of automatic attitudes: Combating automatic prejudice with images of admired and disliked individuals. *Journal of Personality and Social Psychology, 81(5)*, 800-814.

Irene V. Blair and colleagues. (2001). Imagining stereotypes away: The moderation of implicit stereotypes through mental imagery. *Journal of Personality and Social Psychology, 81(5)*, 828-841.

Brian S. Lowery and Curtis D. Hardin (2001). Social influence effects on automatic racial prejudice. *Journal of Personality and Social Psychology, 81(5)*, 842-855.

30. Keith J. Holyoak & Paul Thagard (1995). *Mental Leaps: Analogy in Creative Thought*. Cambridge, MA: MIT Press.

31. Ackerman, Diane (2004). *An Alchemy of Mind: The Marvel and Mystery of the Brain*. New York: Scribner [p. 18].

32. Keith J. Holyoak & Paul Thagard (1995). *Mental Leaps: Analogy in Creative Thought*. Cambridge, MA: MIT Press (p. 9).

33. MSNBC's "Rita Cosby: Live and Direct" August 8, 2005. The two jurors were Eleanor Cook (age 79) and Ray Hultman (62). They acknowledged that they first thought Jackson was guilty but claimed to have been railroaded into a not-guilty verdict.

34. Aronson, E., Wilson, T. D., & Akert, R. M. (1999). *Social psychology* (3rd ed.). New York: Longman.

35. Kahneman, D. (1995). Varieties of counterfactual thinking. In N. J. Roese & J. M. Olson (Eds.), *What might have been: The social psychology of counterfactual thinking* (pp. 375-396). Mahwah, NJ: Lawrence Erlbaum.

36. Decisional Regret Theory holds specifically that people want to live in a predictable world, yet they regularly face uncertain outcomes from decision choices. Faced with decisions, people experience *anxiety* as they *anticipate choice-regret*. The communicative dynamic of Decisional Regret Theory (DERT) is the production, sharing, and reconstruction of *predecisional imaginary narratives* that allow alternative decisional outcomes to be anticipated. DERT predicts a type of shared communication in groups (counterfactual storytelling), under specific circumstances (anticipation of making a meaningful decision). It further predicts responses of other group members: (a) reproducing the story, (b) altering the story, (c) creating an alternative story, or (d) disconfirming the story. Exemplars of counterfactual communication during jury decision making are offered, together with a model describing the emergence of group counterfactual storytelling.

DERT emerged from a study of jury deliberations, reported in: Sunwolf (in press). Decisional regret theory: Reducing the anxiety about uncertain outcomes during group decision making through shared counterfactual storytelling. *Communication Studies*.

37. *"Binge Thinking"* was a hip hop music album (Crest, 2003), containing 17 "think pieces" and featuring Maspyke and J. Sands of the Lone Catalysts; the track "No More Lady" won second place in the John Lennon songwriting contest of 2003. In March of 2005, a documentary of the same name (*"Binge Thinking"*) was released by BBC Wales as part of a social action campaign about risky single occasion alcohol drinking. The words are an intriguing linguistic tool.

38. Juries were first televised in the United States in 1986 when the PBS program *Frontline* covered the criminal trial of a defendant charged with gun possession in Milwaukee, Wisconsin. In order to record jury deliberations, two cameramen and a soundman were inside the jury room throughout the jury's decision-making task. The program was entitled, "Inside the Juryroom." The video may be purchased at www.pbs.org/wgbh/pages/frontline/twenty/programs/1986.htm

39. It is only fair to note that judges and attorneys also engage in binge-thinking (pre-trial, during trial, and post-trial). It can be argued, in fact, that if you are not prone to frequent bouts of binge-thinking, you probably are not practicing trial advocacy. You chose something else. Appellate courts force us to re-engage in binge-thinking long after the trial is over. Some appellate opinions are rich examples of literary binge-thinking.

40. Capra, Fritjof (1988). *Uncommon Wisdom: Conversations with Remarkable People*. New York: Bantam. [pages 76-77]

41. *'The Neurocognitive Self' in The Science of The Mind*, Robert Solso and Dominic Massaro (Eds.) (1995) Oxford University Press [page 229].

42. Pradeep Soporty & James Price Dillard (2002). The persuasive effects of metaphor: A meta-analysis. *Human Communication Research, 28(3)*, 382-419.

43. Glucksberg, S., Gildea, P., & Bookin, H. (1982). On understanding nonliteral speech: Can people ignore metaphors? *Journal of Verbal Learning and Verbal Behaviour, 21*, 85-98.

Glucksberg, S., & Keysar, B. 91990). Understanding metaphorical comparisons: Beyond similarity. *Psychological Review, 97*, 3-18.

44. Gentner, Dedre & Jeziorski, Michael (1993). 'The shift from metaphor to analogy in Western science' in *Metaphor and Thought*, edited by Andrew Ortony (2nd Ed.). Cambridge University Press [page 447].

45. Pinker, Steven (1997). *How The Mind Works*. London: The Softback [page 355].

46. The relationship of metaphor to other figures of speech: A **simile** makes the comparison explicit with a word such as "like," "as," or "than." **Metonymy** is the substitution of a closely related word for the intended subject and does not transfer qualities from one word to another; rather, it uses an existing association to draw a link between words ("The White House issued a statement yesterday," intead of "The President issued a statement yesterday."). **Synecdoche** are expressions that use a part to stand for the whole (or the whole to stand for the part), for example, "Look at his new *wheels*," instead of "Look at new new *car*." An **allegory** is an extended section of prose or verse that carries a meaning or message about something other than its literal subject [see extensive discussion in "Mental Leaps," above, § 2-2].

47. Lakoff, George, & Johnson, Mark (1999). *Philosophy in the Flesh: The Embodied Mind and Its Challenge to Western Thought*. Basic Books [pages 567-568].

48. Lakoff, George, & Johnson, Mark (1999). *Philosophy in the Flesh: The Embodied Mind and Its Challenge to Western Thought*. Basic Books.

49. In *Mental Leaps*, Holyoak and Thagard share a humorous metaphor stretched to analogy that was once used by a sportscaster, who wrote: "Trying to explain baseball to a nonfan is like trying to explain sex to an eight-year-old: no matter how much detail you go into, the response is still, "But why?" It is futile to talk baseball to the uninterested.

50. Robert Stetson Shaw, quoted in James Gleick, 1987, *Chaos: Making a New Science*. New York: Viking (p. 262).

51. Jose Ortega y Gasset was a Spanish philosopher and humanist who lived from 1883 to 1955.

52. John M. Conley (2000). A legal and cultural commentary on the psychology of jury instructions. *Psychology, Public Policy, and Law, 6(3)*, 822-831.

53. Jennifer L. Skeem, & Stephen L. Golding (2001). Describing jurors' personal conceptions of insanity and their relationship to case judgments. *Psychology, Public Policy, and Law, 7(3)*, 561-621.

54. Joel D. Lieberman & Bruce D. Sales (1997). What social science teaches us about the jury instruction process. *Psychology, Public Policy, and Law, 3(4)*, 589-644.

See also Norman J. Finkel (2000). Commonsense justice and jury instructions: Instructive and Reciprocating connections. *Psychology, Public Policy, and Law, 6(3)*, 591-628.

55. Excellent discussion of the *mirror effect* pattern, in which own-race faces yielded a higher proportion of hits and a lower proportion of false alarms, compared with other-race faces. Christian A. Meissner & John C. Brigham (2001). Thirty years of investigating the own-race bias in memory for faces. *Psychology, Public Policy, and Law, 7(1)*, 3-35.

56. Mollie W. Marti & Roselle L. Wissler (2000). Be careful what you ask for: The effect of anchors on personal injury damages awards. *Journal of Experimental Psychology: Applied, 6(2)*, 91-103.

See also an excellent discussion of instructions in personal injury cases on general damages, with specific suggestions: Roselle L. Wissler, Patricia F. Kuehn, & Michael J. Saks (2000). Instructing jurors on general damages in personal injury cases: Problems and possibilities. *Psychology, Public Policy, and Law, 6(3)*, 712-742.

Edith Greene & Brian Bornstein (2000). Precious little guidance: Jury instructions on damage awards. *Psychology, Public Policy, and Law, 6(3)*, 743-768.

57. Allen J. Hart (1995). Naturally occurring expectation effects. *Journal of Personality and Social Psychology, 68(1)*, 109-115.

58. An older case, but often overlooked: Vicki L. Smith (1991). Prototypes in the courtroom: Lay representations of legal concepts. *Journal of Personality and Social Psychology, 61(6)*, 857-872.

59. Olga Nikonova & James R. P. Ogloff (2005). Mock jurors' perceptions of child witnesses: The impact of judicial warning. *Canadian Journal of Behavioural Science, 37(1)*, 1-19.

ENDNOTES

60. Daniel R. Ames (2004). Inside the mind reader's tool kit: Projection and stereotyping in mental state inference. *Journal of Personality and Social Psychology, 87(3)*, 340-353.

61. Jennifer S. Hunt, & Thomas Lee Budesheim (2004). How jurors use and misuse character evidence. *Journal of Applied Psychology, 89(2)*, 347-361.

62. Irwin A. Horowitz, & Kenneth S. Bordens (2002). The effects of jury size, evidence complexity, and note taking on jury process and performance in a civil trial. *Journal of Applied Psychology, 87(1)*, 121-130.

63. Rule 801 permits two exceptions regarding out-of-court statements of a party-opponent or testifying witness. Rule 803 (Hearsay Exceptions, Availability of Declarant Immaterial) recognizes twenty-three specific exceptions and one residual exception. Rule 804 (Hearsay Exceptions, Declarant Unavailable) offers four exceptions and one residual exception.

64. Lucy S. McGough (1999). Hearing and believing hearsay. *Psychology, Public Policy, and Law, 5(2)*, 485-498.

65. Michelle Rae Tuckey & Neil Brewer (2003). The influence of schemas, stimulus ambiguity, and interview schedule on eyewitness memory over time. *Journal of Experimental Psychology: Applied, 9(2)*, 101-118.

66. Sheree T. Kwong See, Hunter G. Hoffman, & Tammy L. Wood (2001). Perceptions of an old female eyewitness: Is the older eyewitness believable? *Psychology and Aging, 16(2)*, 346-350.

67. Edith Greene, Michael Johns, & Alison Smith (2001). The effects of defendant conduct on jury damage awards. *Journal of Applied Psychology, 86(2)*, 228-237. Surpassing the usual extra credit/college student design, this study involved 561 jury-eligible adults ranging in age from 18 to 87 (mean 45), and were screened for jury eligibility. Further, pre-deliberation and post-deliberation data were gathered from individual participants, in addition to the group verdicts.

68. Shari Seidman Diamond, Neil Vidmar, Mary Rose, Leslie Ellis, & Beth Murphy (2003). Juror discussions during civil trials: Studying an Arizona innovation. 45 *Ariz. L. Rev.* 1. These researchers had deliberation videotapes as well as juror questions.

Earlier studies from Arizona reform on discussions, Paul L. Hannaford et al., Permitting Jury Discussions During Trial: Impact of the Arizona Reform, 24 *Law & Hum. Behav.* 359 (2000); Paula L. Hannaford-Agor et al., Speaking Rights: Evaluating Juror Discussions During Civil Trials, 85 *Judicature* 237 (2002).

See also Valerie P. Hans et al., The Arizona Jury Reform Permitting Civil Jury Trial Discussions: The Views of Trial Participants, Judges and Jurors, 32 *U. Mich. J.L. Reform* 349 (1999).

Discussion about the long practice forbidding juror discussion in criminal cases, in *Winebrenner* v. *United States* 147 F.2d 322 (8th Cir. 1945), recognizing the principle that it is improper for jurors to discuss a case prior to its submission to them.

69. Koren, Leonard (1994). *Wabi-Sabi for Artists, Designers, Poets, & Philosophers.* Berkeley, CA: Stone Bridge Press. Leonard Koren was trained as an architect but never built any structures—he resides in both America and Japan and has built, instead, many books.

70. Gold, Taro (2004). *Living Wabi Sabi: The True Beauty of Your Life.* Kansas City, MO: Andrews McMeel Publishing.

71. Barry Schwartz (2004). *The Paradox of Choice: Why More Is Less.* New York: HarperCollins.

WHO IS THE AUTHOR?

DR. SUNWOLF has been fascinated with jurors and their imperfect worlds since her first trial, in 1975. A veteran of many roles within the American justice system (law school faculty, civil litigation attorney, Training Director for Colorado's Public Defender System, trial consultant)—a moment of epiphany during a death penalty trial (about how to touch a juror's heart as well as mind) pushed her back to graduate school, where she completed both Master's and Doctoral degrees in Interpersonal and Group Communication from the University of California, Santa Barbara in 1998. Dr. Sunwolf is now an Associate Professor of Communication at Santa Clara University, California, where she teaches interpersonal relationships, group dynamics, conflict, persuasion, and oral storytelling. An active trial consultant and media trial-analyst, she serves on trial advocacy faculties nationally and teaches at continuing education programs throughout the country. Professor Sunwolf is also a performing storyteller, with corresponding research investigating the pedagogical and persuasive effects of multicultural tales. An expert on jury deliberations and social persuasion, she is the originator of Decisional Regret Theory, which explains how jurors attempt to reduce the anxiety of "anticipated verdict-regret" by creating counterfactual stories. Believing that early group experiences affect adult jurors, she has published studies about the painful dynamics of social exclusion in adolescent peer groups. She has recently been appointed Visiting Professor at Santa Clara University School of Law, teaching a new course, "Jury Law and Strategies"—which may be the first law school course in the nation, devoted solely to *jury thinking*.

JURY THINKING

JURORS—THINKING © 2004 SUNWOLF

The good things about this book have drawn upon the generosity of others—while errors, omissions, or confusions lay entirely at my own doorstep.

Insert a low bow of respect
[here]
to all jurors
who tell us their stories during voir dire,
who listen to their hearts
as well as to the testimony,
and who make the decisions.

Sunwolf
Santa Clara, California
August 2005

INDEX

A

ABA 2005 principles for juries and jury trials, § 5-2(a), Appendix.
    reform structures missing from ABA principles, § 5-2(b).

Advertisements.
    mental filters.
        jurors' TiVo minds, illustration, § 1-2(a).

Age stereotyping.
    blink judgment, implicit associations, § 2-1(d).
    juror thinking about witness memory.
        structures that influence thinking, § 5-1(k).

Analogies.
    basic factors for successful analogies, § 2-2(a).
    mental leaps, § 2-2.
    pre-trial preparation, § 2-2(b).
    purposes, § 2-2(a).

Anxiety.
    juror flipping, effect, § 3-1.

Athletes.
    blink judgment, nonjurors, § 2-1(c).

B

Back talking.
    biology of beliefs, § 1-1.

Beliefs.
    biology of beliefs, § 1-1.
    digital recording, jurors' minds compared, § 1-2.
    God words and devil words, § 4-1.
    religious beliefs, § 1-3.
        God and science, thinking regarding, § 1-3(b).

Binge-thinking, § 3-4.
    binge drinking, compared, § 3-4.
    binge-thinking hangover, § 3-4(b).
    how they occur, § 3-4(a).

Binge-thinking, cont'd.
  intervention, § 3-4(c).
  juror thinking binges, effects generally, § 3-4(a).
  variables that contribute, § 3-4(a).

Biology of beliefs, § 1-1.

Biology of disagreement or argument.
  juror flipping, effect, § 3-1.

Bird watchers.
  blink judgment, nonjurors, § 2-1(c).

Black Muslims.
  religious beliefs of jurors, § 1-3.

Blink judgment, § 2-1.
  disabling juror blink, § 2-1(b).
  ick factor, § 2-1(a).
  implicit association interactive test (IAT test), § 2-1(d).
  issue-specific blink, § 2-1(d).
  juror blink, § 2-1(b).
  nonjurors, § 2-1(c).
  voir dire, § 2-1(e).

Buddhism.
  religious beliefs, impact on persuasion, § 1-3(a).

By-passed regret, § 3-2.

C

Character evidence.
  use and misuse.
    structures that influence thinking, § 5-1(h).

Charismatics.
  religious beliefs, impact on persuasion, § 1-3(a).

Childhood devil words, § 4-1.

Christianity.
  religious beliefs of jurors, effect, § 1-3.

Communication culture amongst jurors.
  juror flipping, § 3-1.

INDEX

Community of jurors.
    binge-thinking, § 3-4.

Conceptual system.
    metaphoric thinking, § 4-2.

Conscious attitudes.
    blink judgment, implicit associations, § 2-1(d).

Consequences.
    if-only thinking, § 3-3.

Counterfactual thinking.
    verdict regret, § 3-3.

Courtroom design.
    seating assignments.
        reform structures missing from ABA principles, § 5-2(b).
    structures that influence thinking, § 5-1.
    table, elimination.
        reform structures missing from ABA principles, § 5-2(b).

Cursillo.
    religious beliefs, impact on persuasion, § 1-3(a).

D

Damage awards.
    defendant conduct, effect.
        structures that influence thinking, § 5-1(l).

Death penalty cases.
    Roman Catholic jurors, impact, § 1-3.

Defendant conduct.
    damage awards, effect.
        structures that influence thinking, § 5-1(l).

Deliberations.
    juror flipping, § 3-1.
    religious beliefs, effect, § 1-3(a).
    re-thinking.
        juror flipping, § 3-1.

Digital recording, jurors' minds compared, § 1-2.
    mental filters, § 1-2(a).
    mental short cuts, § 1-2(a).
    message overload, § 1-2(a).
    search, record and fast forward, § 1-2(a).
    teaching jurors how to use, § 1-2(b).

Disability.
    blink judgment, implicit associations, § 2-1(d).

Disgusting evidence.
    ick factor.
        blink judgment, § 2-1(a).

Distractions.
    blink judgment, jurors, § 2-1(b).

E

Evangelicalism.
    religious beliefs, impact on persuasion, § 1-3(a).

Expectation, effects.
    structures that influence thinking, § 5-1(e).

Eyewitnesses.
    juror thinking about witness memory.
        structures that influence thinking, § 5-1(k).

F

Foreperson.
    jury reform, elimination.
        reform structures missing from ABA principles, § 5-2(b).

Fundamentalism.
    religious beliefs, impact on persuasion, § 1-3(a).

G

Gender.
    blink judgment, implicit associations, § 2-1(d).

INDEX

God words and devil words, § 4-1.

Group dynamics.
juror flipping, effect, § 3-1.

H

Hasidism.
religious beliefs, impact on persuasion, § 1-3(a).

Hearsay evidence.
structures that influence thinking, § 5-1(j).

Hunches.
mental shortcuts, § 2-1.

Hung juries.
juror flipping, effect, § 3-1.

I

Ick factor.
blink judgment, § 2-1(a).
neutralizing bad facts, § 2-1(a).

If-only thinking, § 3-3.

Imagination.
mental leaps, § 2-2.

Imperfect thinking.
machine-thinking, § 6-1.
paradox, § 6-3.
wabi-sabi minds, § 6-2.

Implicit association interactive test (IAT test).
blink judgment, § 2-1(d).

Impressions.
theory of thin slices.
blink judgment, jurors, § 2-1(b).

Islam.
   religious beliefs, impact on persuasion, § 1-3(a).
   Sufism.
      religious beliefs, impact on persuasion, § 1-3(a).

J

Jackson, Michael.
   criminal trial.
      juror flipping, example, § 3-1.

Jehovah's Witness.
   religious beliefs of jurors, § 1-3.

Judaism.
   Hasidism.
      religious beliefs, impact on persuasion, § 1-3(a).
   Kabbalah.
      religious beliefs, impact on persuasion, § 1-3(a).

Judicial warnings during trial.
   effect.
      structures that influence thinking, § 5-1(f).

Juror flipping, § 3-1.

Juror regret, § 3-1.
   binge-thinking.
      binge-think hangover, § 3-4(a).
      intervention, § 3-4(c).
   by-passed regret, § 3-2.
   counterfactual thinking, § 3-3.
   if-only thinking, § 3-3.
   ignoring, § 3-2.
   regret contagion, § 3-3.
   restorying, § 3-3.

Jury instructions.
   complex instructions.
      binge-thinking, variables that contribute, § 3-4(a).
   juror flipping, addressing causes, § 3-1.
   structures that influence thinking, § 5-1(a).
   toxic talk, identifying, § 3-1.

INDEX

Jury reform, § 5-2.
    ABA 2005 principles for juries and jury trials, § 5-2(a), Appendix.
        reform structures missing from ABA principles, § 5-2(b).
    foreperson, elimination, § 5-2(b).
    seating assignments, § 5-2(b).
    table, elimination, § 5-2(b).

Jury studies.
    structures that influence thinking, § 5-1.

K

Kabbalah.
    religious beliefs, impact on persuasion, § 1-3(a).

L

Legal concepts.
    lay representations of legal concepts.
        structures that influence thinking, § 5-1(e).

Lengthy trial.
    binge-thinking.
        variables that contribute, § 3-4(a).

Listening skills.
    mental filters, mental shortcuts and message overload.
        jurors' TiVo minds, § 1-2(a).
    TiVo thinking.
        teaching jurors how to use their TiVo brains, § 1-2(b).

M

Machine-thinking.
    imperfect thinking, § 6-1.

Major harm.
    binge-thinking.
        variables that contribute, § 3-4(a).

Media coverage.
    binge-thinking.
        variables that contribute, § 3-4(a).
    juror regret, factors contributing, § 3-1.

Memory.
    juror thinking about witness memory.
        structures that influence thinking, § 5-1(k).

Mental filters.
    jurors' TiVo minds, § 1-2(a).
        helping jurors identify mental pre-settings, § 1-2(b).
    religious beliefs.
        persuasion, religious thinking, impact, § 1-3(a).

Mental leaps, § 2-2.
    analogies.
        basic factors for successful analogies, § 2-2(a).
        pre-trial preparation, § 2-2(b).
        purposes, § 2-2(a).

Mental rulers.
    religious beliefs.
        determining value system of jurors, § 1-3(a).

Mental shortcuts.
    blink judgment, § 2-1.
    jurors' TiVo minds, § 1-2(a).
        helping jurors identify mental pre-settings, § 1-2(b).
    mental leaps, § 2-2.
    metaphoric thinking.
        complex metaphoric phrases, § 4-2(d).
    thinking unaware, § 2-1.

Mental states.
    structures that influence thinking, § 5-1(g).

Message overload.
    jurors' TiVo minds, § 1-2(a).

Metaphoric thinking, § 4-2(a).
    binge-thinking intervention, § 3-4(c).
    complex metaphoric phrases, § 4-2(d).
    emotional metaphors.
        types of metaphoric talk, § 4-2(c).
    God words and devil words, § 4-1.

Metaphoric thinking, cont'd.
  metaphors generally, § 4-2.
  patchwork metaphors, § 4-2(d).
  sensory metaphors.
    types of metaphoric talk, § 4-2(c).
  speaking in metaphors, § 4-2(b).
  types of metaphoric talk, § 4-2(c).
  types of metaphors, § 4-2(d).

Military.
  blink judgment, nonjurors, § 2-1(c).

Mind-spinning, § 2-1.

Motive.
  dislike as motivating factor.
    blink judgment, nonjurors, § 2-1(c).

Multiple acts of wrongdoing.
  binge-thinking.
    variables that contribute, § 3-4(a).

Multiple issues.
  binge-thinking.
    variables that contribute, § 3-4(a).

Multiple verdicts.
  binge-thinking, variables that contribute, § 3-4(a).

N

Neural excitement.
  biology of beliefs, § 1-1.

Nonunanimous juries.
  ignoring regret, § 3-2.

Notetaking.
  structures that influence thinking, § 5-1(i).

P

Paganism.
  religious beliefs, impact on persuasion, § 1-3(a).

Paradox.
   imperfect thinking, § 6-3.
   paradox of choice, § 6-3(b).
   unavoidable paradox, § 6-3(a).
      binge-thinking intervention, § 3-4(c).

Patients.
   blink judgment, nonjurors, § 2-1(c).

Pentecostals.
   religious beliefs, impact on persuasion, § 1-3(a).
   religious beliefs of jurors, § 1-3.

Perceptions.
   mental filters.
      jurors' TiVo minds, § 1-2(a).

Personal injury damage awards.
   structures that influence thinking, § 5-1(c).

Persuasion.
   religious beliefs.
      constraints on persuasion, overriding religious beliefs, § 1-3(a).
      using beliefs as markers for framing issues, § 1-3(a).
   religious beliefs, impact, § 1-3(a).

Physicians.
   blink judgment, nonjurors, § 2-1(c).

Presumptions.
   erroneous presumptions.
      blink judgment, jurors, § 2-1(b).

Pre-trial preparation.
   analogies, § 2-2(b).

R

Race.
   blink judgment, implicit associations, § 2-1(d).
   own racial bias.
      structures that influence thinking, § 5-1(b).

INDEX

Regretting the verdict.
  binge-thinking.
    binge-think hangover, § 3-4(a).
    intervention, § 3-4(c).
    variables that contribute, § 3-4(a).
  by-passed regret, § 3-2.
  counterfactual thinking, § 3-3.
  if-only thinking, § 3-3.
  ignoring, § 3-2.
  regret contagion, § 3-3.
  restorying, § 3-3.
  re-thinking.
    juror flipping, § 3-1.

Religious beliefs, § 1-3.
  blink judgment, implicit associations, § 2-1(d).
  God and science, thinking regarding, § 1-3(b).
  God words and devil words, § 4-1.
  persuasion.
    constraints on persuasion, overriding religious beliefs, § 1-3(a).
    religious thinking, impact, § 1-3(a).
    using beliefs as markers for framing issues, § 1-3(a).
  questions on juror's religious practices, § 1-3(b).
  value system, impact, § 1-3(a).

Repulsive evidence.
  ick factor.
    blink judgment, § 2-1(a).

Restorying.
  verdict regret, § 3-3.

Re-thinking.
  binge-thinking, § 3-4.
  if-only thinking, § 3-3.
  juror flipping, § 3-1.
  juror regret, ignoring, § 3-2.

Retrials.
  juror flipping, effect, § 3-1.

Roman Catholics.
  Cursillo.
    religious beliefs, impact on persuasion, § 1-3(a).
  religious beliefs of jurors, effect, § 1-3.

S

Scientific evidence.
God and science, thinking regarding, § 1-3(b).

Scruples.
religious beliefs of jurors, § 1-3.

Seating assignments.
jury reform.
reform structures missing from ABA principles, § 5-2(b).

Sexual orientation.
blink judgment, implicit associations, § 2-1(d).

Skin tone.
blink judgment, implicit associations, § 2-1(d).

Snap judgments.
blink judgment, § 2-1. See BLINK JUDGMENT.

Speed dating.
voir dire, compared, § 2-1(e).

Sufism.
religious beliefs, impact on persuasion, § 1-3(a).

Symbolic thinking.
childhood devil words, § 4-1.
complex metaphoric phrases, § 4-2(d).
emotional metaphors.
types of metaphoric talk, § 4-2(c).
God words and devil words, § 4-1.
metaphor and thought, § 4-2.
metaphoric thinking, § 4-2(a).
patchwork metaphors, § 4-2(d).
sensory metaphors.
types of metaphoric talk, § 4-2(c).
speaking in metaphors, § 4-2(b).
types of metaphoric talk, § 4-2(c).
types of metaphors, § 4-2(d).

INDEX

T

Thinking unaware.
    blink judgment, § 2-1.
    mental leaps, § 2-2.
    mind-spinning, § 2-1.

Thin slices, theory of.
    blink judgment, jurors, § 2-1(b).
    mental shortcuts, § 2-1.

Thought-purging.
    binge-thinking, § 3-4.

Threats.
    juror flipping, effect, § 3-1.

TiVo, jurors' minds compared, § 1-2.
    mental filters, § 1-2(a).
    mental short cuts, § 1-2(a).
    message overload, § 1-2(a).
    search, record and fast forward, § 1-2(a).
    teaching jurors how to use, § 1-2(b).

Toxic talk.
    juror flipping, effect, § 3-1.

U

Unconscious attitudes.
    blink judgment, implicit associations, § 2-1(d).

V

Value system.
    religious beliefs, impact, § 1-3(a).

Verdict regret, § 3-1.
    binge-thinking.
        binge-think hangover, § 3-4(a).
        intervention, § 3-4(c).
    by-passed regret, § 3-2.
    counterfactual thinking, § 3-3.

Verdict regret, cont'd.
   if-only thinking, § 3-3.
   ignoring, § 3-2.
   regret contagion, § 3-3.
   restorying, § 3-3.

Voir dire.
   blink judgment, jurors, § 2-1(b).
   blink judgment, use, § 2-1(e).
   religious beliefs of jurors, § 1-3.
   speed dating, compared, § 2-1(e).
   TiVo thinking.
      teaching jurors how to use their TiVo brains, § 1-2(b).
   toxic talk, identifying, § 3-1.

W

Wabi-sabi minds.
   imperfect thinking, § 6-2.

Warnings.
   judicial warnings during trial, effect.
      structures that influence thinking, § 5-1(f).

Weapons.
   blink judgment, implicit associations, § 2-1(d).

Weight.
   blink judgment, implicit associations, § 2-1(d).

Wicca.
   religious beliefs, impact on persuasion, § 1-3(a).

Witnesses.
   juror thinking about witness memory.
      structures that influence thinking, § 5-1(k).

Z

Zen.
   religious beliefs, impact on persuasion, § 1-3(a).

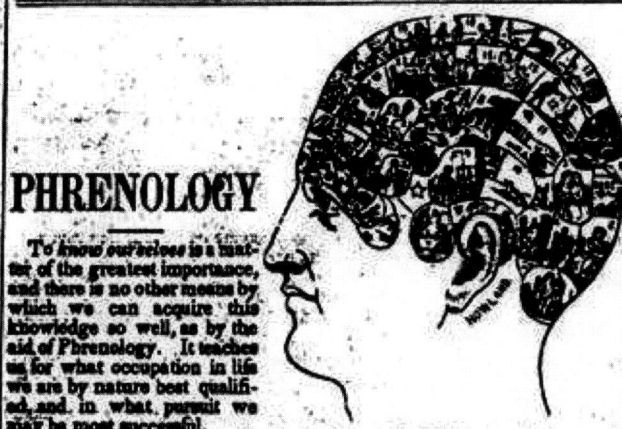

Sell your cleverness
and purchase, instead,
bewilderment.

—Victor Frankel

---

*Advertisement for The Phrenological Cabinet *from Barnum's American Museum Illustrated* (New York, 1850).

Notes